Drupal 7 Multilingual Sites

A hands-on, practical guide for configuring your
Drupal 7 website to handle all languages for your
site users

Kristen Pol

BIRMINGHAM - MUMBAI

Drupal 7 Multilingual Sites

First published: April 2012

Production Reference: 1110412

Published by Packt Publishing Ltd.
Livery Place
35 Livery Street
Birmingham B3 2PB, UK.

ISBN 978-1-84951-818-5

www.packtpub.com

Cover Image by Kristen Pol (coverimage@kristen.org)

Credits

Author
Kristen Pol

Reviewers
Gábor Hojtsy

Jose Reyero

Acquisition Editor
Sarah Cullington

Technical Editors
Veronica Fernandes

Vishal D'souza

Project Coordinators
Yashodhan Dere

Jovita Pinto

Proofreader
Aaron Nash

Indexer
Monica Ajmera Mehta

Graphics
Manu Joseph

Production Coordinator
Prachali Bhiwandkar

Cover Work
Prachali Bhiwandkar

About the Author

Kristen Pol grew up as the youngest sister to five brothers in a small town in rural Central California. After high school and a few community colleges, she earned a BA degree in mathematics and physics at UC Santa Cruz in 1994 and an MSEE at Stanford University in 1995. After college, she worked as a Systems Engineer at Hewlett Packard and then as a Java Application Architect at a web consulting company in downtown Santa Cruz, California, during the dot-com boom.

She started her own software business in 2001. Initially, she focused on Java applications, but in 2004 Drupal changed her life. Starting with version 4, she got hooked on Drupal development and now she focuses pretty much exclusively on Drupal and search engine optimization (SEO). She works with a wide variety of clients throughout North America. She enjoys working on challenging websites that require custom programming. Some of her more notable Drupal projects include boomboomcards.com (social kindness game), naturebridge.org (non-profit bringing kids to nature), thesoundpost.com (Canadian classical instrument shop), and boomerangproject.com (school transition programs).

She is very active in the Drupal community. She has authored contributed modules including Featured Content and SEO Friend, regularly attends the Santa Cruz Drupal user group meetings, improves drupal.org documentation, gives talks at Drupal camps and events, and helps out on the Drupal forums and issue queues. When she's not doing Drupal, she enjoys photography, travel, hiking, and spending time with her husband and two sons in beautiful Santa Cruz. Feel free to contact her at kristen.org/contact.

Acknowledgement

First, I'd like to say a very BIG thank you to Gábor Hojtsy and Jose Reyero for answering my questions and reviewing the book, and to Gábor for letting me use some of his helpful illustrations. These two have contributed an enormous amount of time and effort into improving the Drupal localization process. I'll buy you both a beer at the next DrupalCon!

A special thanks to Aimee Degnan and John Storey for giving useful feedback on the book, and to my local Drupal community, particularly the Santa Cruz user group members who beta tested the book exercises, namely, Linda Donohue, Paul Ferlito, Craig Harris, Mary Edith Ingraham, Jacob Miller, Forest Monsen, Murias O'Ceallagh, Darren Odden, Scott Patterson, Heather Reed, Darryl Richman, Don Skaggs, Rob Thorne, and Julia van der Wyk.

I'm also grateful to my very supportive husband, Josh Deutsch, and to my two wacky boys, Jacob and Aaron. Jacob said that I should mention here that "they didn't annoy me so that I could write the book." Well, at least that shows he had good intentions. I'm exceedingly lucky to have Cerise Cazet, an awesome kid-sitter (and video games for when she's not available!).

Next, I would like to thank the Drupal community at large for providing an interesting and fun environment for being a geek and for creating cool websites. I can't imagine working with any other framework. To keep things succinct, I haven't included the names of the wonderful module creators and maintainers in the book, but you know you rock!

Last of all, I'd like to give thanks to the people at Packt for making this happen. This is my first book and I've learned a lot.

Oh! And, thanks to *you* for reading this.

About the Reviewers

Gábor Hojtsy is an open source enthusiast and contributor, most active as a Drupal developer, working with and on the open source project itself at Acquia. He started off contributing to open source in 2000 when he became an active contributor to the PHP Documentation team. He became the lead to that team and the php.net website team for years. He technically edited the first Hungarian PHP developer book, led courses on web technologies, and co-organized various PHP and generic web development conferences. He started working with and on Drupal in 2003, and became devoted to the multilingual functionality and sometimes the lack thereof. He has been an active contributor ever since, and was the co-organizer of the international DrupalCon Szeged 2008. He is an active maintainer for Drupal 6, the initiator of `localize.drupal.org`, Drupal's software localization site, and lead to the Drupal 8 Multilingual Initiative.

When not geeking out, he is passionate about singing, music, and amateur acting, especially when these are all combined.

Jose Reyero has been working on web development for more than 10 years. He is a long time Drupal contributor and the original author and maintainer of Internationalization and some other Drupal modules. He currently works as a freelance consultant and Drupal developer in León, Spain.

www.PacktPub.com

Support files, eBooks, discount offers and more

You might want to visit www.PacktPub.com for support files and downloads related to your book.

Did you know that Packt offers eBook versions of every book published, with PDF and ePub files available? You can upgrade to the eBook version at www.PacktPub.com and as a print book customer, you are entitled to a discount on the eBook copy. Get in touch with us at service@packtpub.com for more details.

At www.PacktPub.com, you can also read a collection of free technical articles, sign up for a range of free newsletters and receive exclusive discounts and offers on Packt books and eBooks.

http://PacktLib.PacktPub.com

Do you need instant solutions to your IT questions? PacktLib is Packt's online digital book library. Here, you can access, read and search across Packt's entire library of books.

Why Subscribe?

- Fully searchable across every book published by Packt
- Copy and paste, print and bookmark content
- On demand and accessible via web browser

Free Access for Packt account holders

If you have an account with Packt at www.PacktPub.com, you can use this to access PacktLib today and view nine entirely free books. Simply use your login credentials for immediate access.

I dedicate this book to my parents, Merleigh and Bill Jones, and to the memory of my dad, A. John Pol. I love you.

Table of Contents

Preface

Recent estimates show at least 1.5 million websites run on Drupal, which calculates to roughly two percent of all sites. Drupal is used to create personal, business, government, and educational websites including high-profile ones such as `whitehouse.gov`, `duke.edu`, and `economist.com`. Drupal adoption is following a very positive trend; last year alone, the number of Drupal websites increased by more than 33 percent.

Drupal's default installation is in English. But, as you'll soon see, it can be configured to handle other languages as well. Creating a multilingual website expands your audience, and studies have shown that users are more likely to buy products and services on a website when content is presented in their native language. Coupled with the fact that there are many more non-English native speakers than English native speakers, you should see the full value of creating a site that supports other languages.

After working through the book exercises, you will have the skills needed to create a rich and robust multilingual Drupal 7 website. Enjoy!

What this book covers

Chapter 1, Multilingual Overview, Use Cases, and Modules, starts by exploring issues, considerations, and example use cases for multilingual websites. Then, to get more familiar with the topic, technical terminology, a Drupal architecture overview, and a preview of Drupal 7 modules are covered.

Chapter 2, Setting up the Basics: Languages, UI Translation, and System Settings, gets us set up with a test site, so new languages can be added and detected. With languages in place, the chapter addresses Drupal interface and string translation as well as general system configuration such as countries, dates, and variables.

Chapter 3, Working with Content, is dedicated to handling content translation using two different methods, namely, node translation and field translation. Use cases, trade-offs, and issues are discussed for both methods. The chapter includes how to work with built-in content pages such as the default home page.

Chapter 4, Configuring Blocks, Menus, Taxonomy, and Views, deals with configuring these standard Drupal components. Language-independent, language-specific, and multilingual configurations are handled, and implications of node-translated versus field-translated content are discussed.

Chapter 5, Panels, SEO, and More!, goes into advanced topics including Panels, SEO, translation management, theming, and module development.

Appendix, Modules, Resources, and Getting Involved, provides a list of modules used in the book as well as additional multilingual modules and a handy overview table on key module usage. Other resources provided include online documentation, forums, ways to get involved, and plans for Drupal 8.

What you need for this book

For the book exercises, you will need to choose from the following options:

- Use an existing Drupal 7 website
- Create a Drupal 7 website from scratch (drupal.org/project/drupal)
- Use the Localized Drupal Distribution (drupal.org/project/l10n_install)
- Use the demo installation profile (drupal.org/project/multilingual_book_demo)

Who this book is for

If you know the Drupal basics (such as creating content types, blocks, and menus) and want to create a multilingual website for yourself, your company, or your clients, then this book is for you. This book was beta tested by a few "newbie" Drupalers and they were able to go through the exercises without much difficulty.

This book is also very valuable for experienced Drupalers who are new to creating multilingual websites. There are many things to configure and the online documentation is scattered and incomplete. By working through this book, you will learn the intricacies of setting up a multilingual Drupal site, which will save you a lot of time and headache.

Before you start

You are highly encouraged to read this section before you continue with *Chapter 1, Multilingual Overview, Use Cases, and Modules.*

Exercise workflow tips

The book is written as a step-by-step tutorial. It is best to work through the exercises in order. If you do jump ahead, just keep in mind that you might need to install and configure additional modules that were addressed in earlier exercises.

It is also recommended that you disable the Overlay module when working through the exercises for a simpler workflow. In many cases, you will need to flush all caches after each configuration to ensure the system is using the latest settings. When something doesn't work as expected, flush the caches and check again.

Working with modules

The module versions used for the book exercises are listed on the demo installation profile project page (`drupal.org/project/multilingual_book_demo`). These versions are bundled with the demo installation profile software. But, you do not need to use the installation profile to work through the book exercises. If you use different versions of the modules, just remember that you might experience different behavior than what is shown in the book exercises. If any functionality changes drastically, then notes will be added to the errata at `kristen.org/errata`.

The Drupal Internationalization module, used heavily in the book, is a package of many submodules. If an exercise explains installing a module from the Internationalization package, then you only need to download the package once but you'll still need to enable the submodule that is listed.

Extra topics

A few topics that were not included in the book due to space constraints are available at `kristen.org/extra`, so you are encouraged to look there before diving into the chapters. In particular, there is a very useful table for seeing how to access the various translation features at `kristen.org/accesstable`.

Conventions

In this book, you will find a number of styles of text that distinguish between different kinds of information. Here are some examples of these styles, and an explanation of their meaning.

Code words in text are shown as follows: "Drupal requires modules and themes to use the t() function for text that will be displayed in the UI."

A block of code is set as follows:

```
$conf['locale_custom_strings_en'][''] = array(
  'Taxonomy' => 'Categories',
  'Taxonomy term' => 'Category term',
);
```

When we wish to draw your attention to a particular part of a code block, the relevant lines or items are set in bold:

```
if (function_exists('i18n_string')) {
  $name = i18n_string($key, $name);
}
```

New terms and **important words** are shown in bold. Words that you see on the screen, in menus or dialog boxes for example, appear in the text like this: "Click on **Save**".

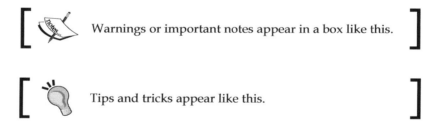

Warnings or important notes appear in a box like this.

Tips and tricks appear like this.

Reader feedback

Feedback from our readers is always welcome. Let us know what you think about this book—what you liked or may have disliked. Reader feedback is important for us to develop titles that you really get the most out of.

To send us general feedback, simply send an e-mail to feedback@packtpub.com, and mention the book title through the subject of your message.

If there is a topic that you have expertise in and you are interested in either writing or contributing to a book, see our author guide on www.packtpub.com/authors.

Customer support

Now that you are the proud owner of a Packt book, we have a number of things to help you to get the most from your purchase.

Errata

Although we have taken every care to ensure the accuracy of our content, mistakes do happen. If you find a mistake in one of our books—maybe a mistake in the text or the code—we would be grateful if you would report this to us. By doing so, you can save other readers from frustration and help us improve subsequent versions of this book. If you find any errata, please report them by visiting http://www.packtpub.com/support, selecting your book, clicking on the **errata submission form** link, and entering the details of your errata. Once your errata are verified, your submission will be accepted and the errata will be uploaded to our website, or added to any list of existing errata, under the Errata section of that title.

Piracy

Piracy of copyright material on the Internet is an ongoing problem across all media. At Packt, we take the protection of our copyright and licenses very seriously. If you come across any illegal copies of our works, in any form, on the Internet, please provide us with the location address or website name immediately so that we can pursue a remedy.

Please contact us at copyright@packtpub.com with a link to the suspected pirated material.

We appreciate your help in protecting our authors, and our ability to bring you valuable content.

Questions

You can contact us at questions@packtpub.com if you are having a problem with any aspect of the book, and we will do our best to address it.

1

Multilingual Overview, Use Cases, and Modules

Drupal is a big system with lots of moving parts. What exactly does it mean to make a multilingual Drupal site? We certainly want to write content in languages other than English. We need blocks and menus to be smart enough so we can use them for different languages. What about Views? Sure, we want it smart too. What about Panels? Yes, of course! What about a seemingly random message string coming from a module we just installed? What about the Drupal UI itself? And so on and so forth.

As you can see, we have a lot of things that need configuring if we want a fully multilingual Drupal website. This book aims at showing you how to navigate through the myriad of modules, configuration settings, and sometimes not-so-intuitive methodologies to make it happen. The exercises in the book are hands-on and organized to give structure to your localization process.

But before we start our exercises and break into a sweat, we need to understand a few things. This chapter will give you an overview of what it means to build a multilingual site in Drupal 7. We will explore a number of issues and considerations when working with multiple languages, and check out some typical use cases. Then, we'll take a look at some terminology and the different parts of the multilingual Drupal puzzle, namely, interface, content, and configuration. The chapter concludes with a preview of the modules we'll use in the coming chapters.

Considerations and use cases

Just like there is no one way to build a regular website, there is no one way to build a multilingual website. Every site is different and has its own use cases and multilingual demands. Check out `amnesty.org`, `drupalcampmontreal.com`, `wunderkraut.com`, `reyero.net`, and `thesoundpost.com` as some unique examples of multilingual Drupal websites.

Different types of language support

You can use as much of Drupal's language support as you need. If you simply want a website that is only shown in German with no English text and no translations, then you can certainly do that. Or, if you want to support content in several languages but none of the content will be translated, you can do that too. For the book exercises, we will be building a fully multilingual site that includes translation. The next figure shows the different levels of language support you might need depending on your site's use cases:

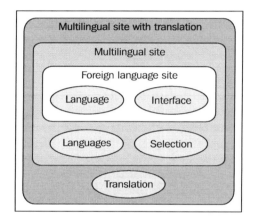

Some things to think about

There are always plenty of things to worry about when designing a website. When you decide to make your site multilingual, the list just gets bigger. This section is not meant to be an exhaustive compilation of everything you need to be thinking about before diving in, but it should help to get you started. We will consider many of these items as we work through our hands-on exercises:

- Should you use a domain, a sub-domain, or a directory per language?
- Do you need translations of all content in all languages?
- If there isn't a translation available, should it show the source content?
- Will translations be done in-house or outsourced and by one person or a team?
- Do you have special e-commerce needs while dealing with taxation or currencies?
- Should the admin UI have a different default language from the end-user UI?

- Do any of your languages need **Right-to-Left** (**RTL**) theming support?
- Will the navigation be different for each language?
- Has the Drupal UI been mostly translated for your chosen languages?
- What translation methods make sense for the site content?

Example use cases

Although there are many ways you can create a multilingual site based on your language needs, the following are some examples to get you thinking more about Drupal's language support.

Simple blog site

Jacob is a writer and has his own website where he blogs about his life and his work. He is fluent in English and Italian, and has a family in Italy where he often goes on vacations. He writes articles in English or Italian depending on the subject. He sometimes translates the blogs so that they are available in both languages, but not always. Jacob does freelance work in the United States. So his work-related content only needs to be in English. He is the sole user for his website but he allows comments to be left in both languages.

Consulting company site

AJ Consulting is a small consulting company in Santa Cruz, California. Drawing from the large Hispanic community in the area, they have several bilingual employees who are fluent in Spanish and English. They specialize in catering to clients who need their services in either language. It is important that they maintain all site content in both languages, so their bilingual employees are in charge of translating content. All content must be approved by the owner prior to being published. The only users of the website are company employees. The general public is not allowed to leave comments anywhere on the site, but they can use the contact form in either English or Spanish.

E-commerce site

Deutsch & Sons is an online store selling educational toys and books for young children. They sell their products internationally but mostly within the United States, Canada, and Mexico. To cater to their international market, they keep their product, store, and customer support content in English, French, and Spanish. They have different shipping and taxation handling based on the shipping country. Deutsch & Sons does not have any staff translators, so they rely on third-party translators who directly modify the site content.

> This example shows functionality based on language and location (country). These are independent features. You might have an English-only site that needs location-based functionality or a multilingual site that does not.

Our demo site

To make things more realistic, our demo site has elements from the examples mentioned previously including blog articles, book content, comments, and user roles that allow more than one content contributor. You can use the demo website or your own site for the book exercises. The book is structured as a step-by-step tutorial. So, for maximum understanding, the best strategy is to work through the chapter exercises in order.

Multilingual Drupal overview

Drupal gets better and better with each release and its multilingual support is no exception. Drupal core provides for basic language support and content translation while contributed modules such as the Internationalization module package pour on the awesome sauce. Also, with Gábor Hojtsy heading up the Drupal 8 Multilingual Initiative (`hojtsy.hu/d8mi`), we know that Drupal 8 is going to be even more amazing.

Speaking the same language... terminology

Before we go multilingual, let's make sure we are all in sync in regards to terminology. You should already be comfortable with the standard Drupal terms before continuing. If words like **node** or **entity** or **taxonomy** aren't clear to you, check out the Drupal glossary at `drupal.org/glossary`. But, there are also lots of fancy words thrown around in the world of internationalization (see, I just used one!). So what exactly do they all mean?

> The word definitions shown next are based on their use in computing and software and, in some cases, are particular to Drupal.

- A **locale** is usually defined as a collection of user information that includes language and location, but the core Locale module only deals with languages.

- A **numeronym** is an abbreviated word where numbers are used to replace letters. Numeronyms are shown in parentheses for some of the terms.

- **Internationalization (i18n)** is the procedure of creating software so that it can handle multiple languages and geographical locations.

- **Localization (L10n)** is the action of updating software so that it can be used for a particular language or region. The numeronym for localization usually starts with an uppercase letter because a lowercase "L" looks like an uppercase letter "I" in some fonts, but module names always use lowercase letters, for example, `l10n_client`.

- **Translation** is the process of converting text from a source language to another language such that the meaning of the text is preserved as much as possible.

- A **translation set** is a collection of objects that includes a source object and all translated versions of the source object. For example, an English source node along with its German and French translated nodes, comprise a translation set.

- The term **interface** (or **user interface** or **UI**) will be used to refer to all the textual information coming from code which may be shown to the user on the website.

- The word **content** will generally be used to represent information that is captured in entities (nodes, comments, users, taxonomy terms, and custom entities).

- The term **config** (or **configuration**) will typically be used to refer to the ad hoc conglomeration of everything that is not considered "interface" or "content."

- The abbreviation **und** comes from the ISO-639 specification and is short for undetermined. You may come across this abbreviation in your database, in code, and in data arrays.

Pieces of the multilingual puzzle

Now that we have our terms clear, let's take a step back and look at the big picture. We will be configuring a lot of different things in the coming chapters. At a high level, these can roughly be separated into the three distinct areas of **interface**, **content**, and **configuration** as defined previously.

The book chapters are roughly divided into these parts with *Chapter 2*, *Setting up the Basics: Languages, UI Translation, and System Settings*, focusing heavily on the user interface, *Chapter 3*, *Working with Content*, on content, *Chapter 4*, *Configuring Blocks, Menus, Taxonomy, and Views*, on standard configuration and *Chapter 5*, *Panels, SEO, and More!*, on advanced configuration.

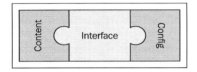

Interface

When you create a Drupal site, you end up with a user interface that has lots of textual information presented to you. Looking at the login block alone, there are the **Username** and **Password** field labels, the **Log in** button text, and a couple of links for creating an account and requesting a password. When we want to use Drupal in another language, all these little bits of text need to be translated into that language and the system needs to know what to do with them.

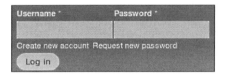

Drupal requires modules and themes to use the `t()` function for text that will be displayed in the UI. (The 't' is short for 'translate'.) If I write a module and have the text `This is the best module EVER!` in it and want that text string to be translated into other languages, then I can use the text as follows:

```
print t('This is the best module EVER!');
```

This lets Drupal know that I want my string to be available for translation. Drupal won't automatically translate the text for you unless it already has that exact string stored away in some other Drupal code and someone has provided the translation.

Fortunately, a lot of Drupal core's UI is already translated into many languages so that part of the battle is won if you want to use one of those languages. You can use the Localized Drupal Distribution install profile (`drupal.org/project/l10n_install`) to make it easier. The trickier part is when contributed modules or your own code have strings in them that aren't yet translated like in the previous example, or you find missing or broken translations in the core interface. This interface translation process will be covered in *Chapter 2*, *Setting up the Basics: Languages, UI Translation, and System Settings*.

Content

When talking about content in Drupal 7, we are mainly thinking about entities (nodes, comments, users, and taxonomy terms). Sure, there are other bits of content floating around the site in views headers, custom block bodies, and panel panes, but we will lump those different non-entity bits in our all-encompassing 'configuration' bucket.

In Drupal 7, entities can have fields (similar to CCK in previous Drupal versions). This has made content translation for nodes more flexible as well as more confusing. In previous versions, if we wanted to translate nodes, we ended up with a separate node for each translation. We can still do this in Drupal 7, but now we can also translate fields with the help of the Entity Translation module where we are only working with one node. In the field translation model, we can translate any of the fields into our various languages. The following figure illustrates the differences between these two methods:

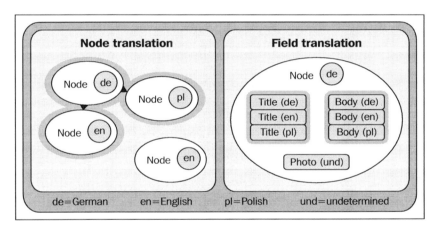

One of the biggest issues with translating nodes in Drupal 7 is that we have to choose between the node translation model and the field translation model for each content type. This is one of the major hot buttons for the Drupal 8 Multilingual Initiative and will definitely be addressed in Drupal 8. To better understand the trade-offs involved, we will work with both of these models in *Chapter 3, Working with Content*.

Although core content translation is only available for nodes, field translation via the Entity Translation module can be used for other core entities (comments, users, and taxonomy terms) and some custom entities. For example, if you have a user **Bio** field or a comment **Internal notes** field, you could choose to translate those fields.

One oddball to mention is taxonomy. You can use field translation for taxonomy term fields and you can also translate vocabularies and terms with the Taxonomy Translation module. The former falls under the "content" area whereas the latter is in the "config" bucket, so it's a bit confusing. These methods will be explored in *Chapter 3*, *Working with Content*, and *Chapter 4*, *Configuring Blocks, Menus, Taxonomy, and Views*.

Configuration

Although interface and content translation are both pretty well-defined and understood, the world of configuration is varied and sometimes complex. There is no configuration API (though that will likely change in Drupal 8), so how we deal with the multitude of config pieces is not very uniform.

Currently, Drupal core doesn't provide much multilingual support beyond the basic foundation, so we end up using a lot of contributed modules. The Internationalization module provides most of the help with 14 submodules. This module has been around since Drupal 4 and is still a lifesaver for Drupal 7. There's talk that much of the Internationalization module package functionality will end up in Drupal 8 core.

Chapter 2, *Setting up the Basics: Languages, UI Translation, and System Settings*, will mainly focus on the UI, but we will also spend time on the configuration for system functionality such as variables, dates, and the contact form. In *Chapter 4*, *Configuring Blocks, Menus, Taxonomy, and Views*, and *Chapter 5*, *Panels, SEO, and More!*, we will work through the multilingual configuration of blocks, menus, taxonomy, and views and then move on to some more advanced topics including panels and SEO.

A look at the modules

In the Drupal community, the phrase "There's a module for that" is often used and for good reason. Currently the drupal.org site boasts of more than 13,000 modules that have been contributed by community members. Searching this multitude of modules for the ones you need isn't easy, but fortunately taxonomy comes to our rescue this time.

The categorization of modules at `drupal.org/project/modules` includes a **Multilingual** category among its options. If we choose that term along with restricting our modules to Drupal 7 versions, then we narrow down our list to only about 50 modules. This is certainly a more manageable number! We won't use all of these in the book, but check out the *Appendix, Modules, Resources, and Getting Involved*, for a list of multilingual modules we will use as well as additional useful modules. The module list includes project page URLs for all modules, so you will know where to find them.

Summary

This chapter has provided us with a broad overview of the language support in Drupal 7. Let's do a quick recap of what we covered.

First, we looked at the different ways to use Drupal's language support, and considered some potential questions to ask before creating a multilingual website. To further our knowledge, we considered a few realistic use cases for different web audiences. We then learned the special terminology associated with the world of Drupal localization.

With our vocabulary enhanced, we moved on to looking at the big pieces of the Drupal 7 multilingual puzzle, namely, interface, content, and configuration. The user interface strings that need translation come from core and contributed modules and themes. For translating content, we narrowed in on data coming from entities. And, for the last piece of the puzzle, we saw that the remaining multilingual configuration involves many elements including handling blocks, menus, taxonomy, and views. The chapter concluded with a preview of the Drupal 7 modules that we'll use very soon.

Now that we understand the big picture, it's time to get to work. In the next chapter, we'll keep ourselves occupied with language settings, interface translation, and general system configuration. If you are ready to go, let's move on and get busy.

2
Setting up the Basics: Languages, UI Translation, and System Settings

In the previous chapter, we got our bearings as we learned about Drupal internationalization at a conceptual level. Now we will get down to business and begin our localization process.

This chapter starts with setting up a test site to use for the book exercises. Once the site is ready, we'll add several new languages and configure language detection so that we can view each language using different URLs. With the detection in place, we will enable a switcher block to easily navigate between each language.

After the language settings are done, we'll move on to translating the Drupal interface. First we will translate manually by grabbing files from `localize.drupal.org`, and then we'll configure the site for automatic updates. Once the contributed translations are in place, we will learn how to add and change translated UI strings as well as how to contribute these translations back to the Drupal community. The last part of the interface translation section deals with changing English strings and reusing strings on other sites.

The final section of the chapter will touch upon several general system configuration areas. We'll update the default country, time zone settings, and date/time formats. The chapter concludes with translating site variables and the general contact fcrm.

Getting up and running

Before we get started, we obviously need a Drupal 7 website to work on. This section gives you two options, namely, roll your own or install the demo.

Using your own site

You can use your own Drupal 7 site. It can be an existing site or one you create from scratch. If you are creating a brand new site and weren't planning on using a particular installation profile, you can get a head start by using the Localized Drupal Distribution install profile at `drupal.org/project/l10n_install`.

It is probably obvious, but it's best to run the site on a development machine and not in a production environment. Once all the basic Drupal core modules are configured, you will also want to set up the following additional modules to get the most out of the exercises:

- **Panels**: A tool for creating pages with custom layouts
- **Pathauto**: Settings for creating path aliases automatically
- **Views**: A tool for creating custom pages and blocks

Using the demo site

If you'd prefer a jump-start, a full demo website can be created using a special install profile, so that you can work through all the book exercises without setting up your own site from scratch.

Instructions for downloading and installing the demo website are included on the Drupal project page available at `drupal.org/project/multilingual_book_demo`. The demo site contains additional modules including the modules listed previously as well as the following:

- **Administration Menu**: Toolbar for quick access to the site configuration
- **Views Bulk Operations**: Extra functionality for Views forms
- **Views Slideshow**: Slideshows of content coming from Views

These modules provide us with a starting point. As more modules are needed for particular exercises, they will be listed so you can add them.

Roles, users, and permissions

Although you might already have multiple users on your test site, for simplicity it will be assumed that you are logged in as the super admin (user ID 1) for the book exercises. The translation management section in *Chapter 5, Panels, SEO, and More!*, will go into more detail on how to deal with roles and permissions.

Working with languages

If we want a multilingual site, the logical first step is to add more languages! In this section, we will add languages to our site, configure how our languages are detected, and set up ways to go between these languages.

Adding languages with the Locale module

Drupal has language support built into the core, but it's not fully turned on by default. If you go to your site right now and navigate to **Configuration | Regional and language**, you will see the **Regional settings** and **Date and time** config pages for configuring default country, time zone, and date/time formats:

1. To get our languages hooked in, let's enable the core module, Locale. Now go back to **Configuration | Regional and language** to see more options:

   Regional settings
   Date and time
   Languages
   Translate interface

2. Click on **Languages** and you'll see we only have **English** in our list so far:

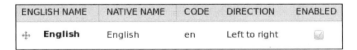

ENGLISH NAME	NATIVE NAME	CODE	DIRECTION	ENABLED
✛ **English**	English	en	Left to right	☑

3. Now let's add a language by clicking on the **Add language** link. You can add a predefined language such as German or you can create a custom language.

4. For our purposes, we will work with predefined languages. So choose a language and click on the **Add language** button.

Drupal will then redirect you to the main language admin page and your new language will be added to the list.

5. Now you can simply repeat the process for each language. In my case, I've added three new languages, namely, **Arabic**, **German**, and **Polish**:

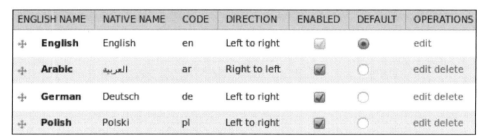

ENGLISH NAME	NATIVE NAME	CODE	DIRECTION	ENABLED	DEFAULT	OPERATIONS
English	English	en	Left to right	☑	◉	edit
Arabic	العربية	ar	Right to left	☑	○	edit delete
German	Deutsch	de	Left to right	☑	○	edit delete
Polish	Polski	pl	Left to right	☑	○	edit delete

The overview table shows the language's name (English and native), its code, and its directionality. The language's direction can be **Left to right** (LTR) or **Right to left** (RTL), with most languages using the former. 'Right to left' just means that you start at the right side of the page and move towards the left side when you are writing. RTL languages include Arabic, Hebrew, and Syriac, which are written in their own alphabets.

You can choose which languages to enable, order them, and set the site default. Links are provided to edit and delete each language. English only has an edit link since it is the system language and cannot be deleted, but English can be disabled if you use a non-English default. If we edit a language, we can modify all the information from the overview table except for the language's code since we need that as a consistent reference string.

Do not change the default language once you have started translating or translations might break.

Several of the book exercises depend on the String Translation module and the String Translation source language must be set correctly or translations might break. Install String Translation from the Internationalization package (`drupal.org/project/i18n`), go to **Configuration | Regional and language | Multilingual settings | Strings**, select the **Source language**, and click on **Save configuration**. Do not change this setting once it's configured.

Detecting languages

We have our languages, so now what? If you click around your site, nothing looks different. That's because we are looking at the English version of the site and we haven't told Drupal how we want to deal with the other languages. We'll do that now.

Navigate to **Configuration | Regional and language | Languages | Detection and selection** and you'll see we have a number of choices available to us:

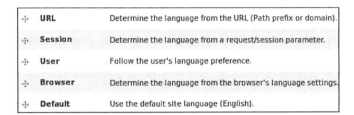

⊹	**URL**	Determine the language from the URL (Path prefix or domain).
⊹	**Session**	Determine the language from a request/session parameter.
⊹	**User**	Follow the user's language preference.
⊹	**Browser**	Determine the language from the browser's language settings.
⊹	**Default**	Use the default site language (English).

The **Default** detection method is enabled for us, but we can also enable the **URL**, **Session**, **User**, and **Browser** options. If you want a cookie-based option, check out the Language Cookie and Locale Cookie modules. Let's go over the core options in more detail.

URL

If you enable this method, users can navigate to URLs such as `example.com/de/news` or `example.com/deutsch/news` (when using the path prefix option) and `example.de/news`, `deutschexample.com/news`, or `deutsch.example.com/news` (when using the domain option). Configuring domains requires web server changes, but using path prefixes does not. This is a common configuration for multilingual sites, and one we'll use shortly.

The language's path prefix can be changed when editing the language. If you want to use path-prefixed URLs, then you should decide on your path prefixes before translating content as changing path prefixes might break links (unless you set up proper redirects). If desired, you can choose one language that does not have any path prefix. This is common for the site's default language. For example, if German is the default language and no path prefix is used, the news page would be accessed as `example.com/news` whereas other languages would be accessed using a path prefix (for example, `example.com/en/news`).

Session

The **Session** option is available if you want to store a user's language preference inside their user session. It was actually proposed by some Drupal community members that this method be removed from the set of choices as it caused a number of issues in other code.

One reason you may not want to use this option is due to the possible inconsistency between the content and the URL language. For example, you could enable both **URL** and **Session** methods and order them so that the **Session** method is first. If a user is at `example.com/de` and if the session is set to French, then the user will see French content even though the URL corresponds with German. My advice is to just skip this one, or, if you need it, at least make sure that it's ordered below the **URL** option.

User

Once the Locale module is enabled, users can specify their preferred language when they edit their account profile. If you enable the **User** method in the detection settings, the user's profile language will be checked when deciding what language to display. Note that the user profile language defaults to the site's default language.

Language

◉ English

○ Arabic (العربية)

○ German (Deutsch)

○ Polish (Polski)

Browser

Users can configure their browsers to specify which languages they prefer. If the **Browser** method is enabled, Drupal will check the browser's request to find out the language setting and use it for the language choice. This option may or may not be useful depending on your site audience.

Default

The default site language is configured on the **Configuration | Regional and language | Languages** settings page, and is used for the **Default** detection method. Although you can't disable this method, you can reorder it if you choose. But, it makes the most sense to keep it at the bottom of the list to use it as the fallback language.

Detection method order

It is important to note that the detection method order is critical to how detection works. If you were to drag the **Default** method to the top of the list, then none of the other methods would be used and the site would only use the default language. Similarly, if you allow a user profile language and drag **User** to top of the list, then the **URL** method would not matter even if it's enabled. Also, if **URL** detection is ordered below **Session**, **User**, and **Browser** options, the user might see a UI language that does not match up with the URL language, which could be confusing.

Make sure to think carefully about the order of these settings. If you use the **URL** method, it's likely you will want it first. The **Default** method should be last. The other detection method positions depend on your preference.

When using path-prefixed URLs, if one language does not have a prefix, then detection for that language will work differently. For example, if the **URL** method is first, then no other detection methods will trigger for any URLs with no path prefix such as `example.com/news` or `example.com/about-us`.

Our choice

For our purposes, let's stick with **URL** detection and use the path-prefix option as this is the easiest to configure (it doesn't require extra domains). This choice will keep our URLs in sync with our interface language, which is also user and SEO-friendly.

1. Check **Enabled** for the **URL** method and press the **Save settings** button.

2. Now click on **Configure** for that method and you'll see options for **Path prefix** and **Domain**. We'll use the default option, that is **Path prefix** (for example, `example.com/de`).

   Don't panic on the next step. You won't see anything different in the UI until we finish our interface translation process later in the chapter.

3. Now change the URL in your browser to include the path prefix for one of your languages. In my case, I'll try German and go to `example.com/de`. You should be able to use the path prefixes for each of your configured languages.

Switching between languages

Most likely you don't want your users to have to manually type in a different URL to switch between languages. Drupal core provides a language switcher block that you can put somewhere convenient for your users.

To use the block, navigate to **Structure | Blocks**, find the **Language switcher (User interface text)** block, position it where you'd like, and save your block settings. The order of the languages in the block is based on the order configured at **Configuration | Regional and language | Languages**. Once enabled, the language switcher block looks like the following screenshot:

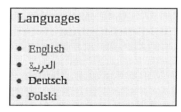

You can now easily switch between your site languages, and the language chosen is highlighted. The UI won't look different when switching until we finish the next section. Two alternatives to the core language switcher block are provided by the Language Switcher and Language Switcher Drop-down modules. Also, if you want country flag icons added next to each language, you can install the Language Icons module.

Interface and string translations

Now that we have our languages configured and can switch between them, we want to start viewing text in these languages. For my site, I chose Arabic, German, and Polish. By going to localize.drupal.org, you can see that these three languages are pretty well supported in Drupal because many of the core UI strings have been translated already.

Take a look to see what progress has been made for your languages. If you want to use a language that hasn't been fully translated, you can always help with the translations yourself and contribute them back to the community. That's what Drupal is all about!

In this section, we'll learn how to translate the UI using the manual process and then by leveraging the Localization Update module. After our interface is in sync with the contributed translations, we will translate new strings into our languages and change existing translations that aren't to our liking. Finally, we'll find out how to send these new translations back to localize.drupal.org so that others can benefit from our hard work.

Translating the interface

For Drupal to know how to translate each interface string, it needs the mapping of the English strings to their translated counterparts. This is handled by using GNU gettext .po files, where po stands for portable object. A .po file looks like the following:

```
#: admin_menu.inc:261
msgid "Enable developer modules"
msgstr "Entwicklermodule aktivieren"
```

The msgid is the English string and the msgstr is the translated version in the target language. The previous example is for a German translation and is in a file called de.po (remember de is the language code for German).

So, what we need to do is grab `.po` files for our site so that Drupal can start translating:

1. Go to `localize.drupal.org` and use the **Quick navigation** to find your language. You will end up on the downloads page for that language where the available translation files are listed. Since version numbers change regularly, grab the latest 7.x version:

Drupal core	5.23	Download (411.42 KB)
Drupal core	6.23	Download (531.29 KB)
Drupal core	7.11	Download (676.37 KB)

2. Click on the **Download** link for **Drupal core** (7.x version) and save your file somewhere handy.

3. Repeat for each language and then navigate to **Configuration | Regional and language | Translate interface**.

4. Now click on the **Import** tab to upload the `.po` files which you have saved. Just import each one separately and assign the correct language when importing:

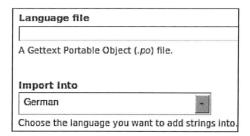

With the `.po` files imported, Drupal now knows how to translate many of the strings in the UI. The overview at **Configuration | Regional and language | Translate interface** shows the translation progress for the site's enabled languages.

LANGUAGE	BUILT-IN INTERFACE
English (built-in)	n/a
Arabic	4350/11431 (38.05%)
German	9482/11431 (82.95%)

Now if I look at the login form with the German interface, the text strings are in German. It's time to see for yourself! Switch between your languages to see the transformation.

If you want to have a different interface language for your administration pages, check out the Administration Language module.

Automatic translation updates

Ok, let's be honest. That was a bit tedious. What if I want to add more languages? What about all my contributed modules that need translation. I, for one, don't want to import each and every .po file for all my modules in all my languages! Fortunately, we don't have to because the Localization Update module comes to our rescue:

admin – language module

pdate module (drupal.org/
ate back to the **Configuration |**
erface page.

e tab and then wait for a few

3. Once the **Update** page loads, you'll see the translation status for your website because the Localization Update module got all that information from `localize.drupal.org`. Cool!

Arabic	panels-7.x-3.0-alpha3.ar.po 📄 06/30/2011 - 15:09	Remote update available ⚠
German	panels-7.x-3.0-alpha3.de.po 📄 06/30/2011 - 15:09	Remote update available ⚠
Polish	panels-7.x-3.0-alpha3.pl.po 📄 06/09/2011 - 14:57	Remote update available ⚠

The rest of our translations can be pulled over at the touch of a button!

4. Click on **Update translations** and wait for a few minutes while Localization Update does all the hard work for you.

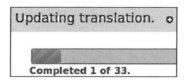

When the update is completed, all your translation status information will change accordingly.

 Some projects might not have translations and translations are only made available for non-development releases, for example, 7.x-1.0 and not 7.x-1.0-dev.

To fully configure Localization Update, check out the config page at **Configuration | Regional and language | Languages | Translation updates**. For example, you can have the module update your site automatically on a daily or weekly schedule. Awesome!

Adding and fixing interface translations

Thanks to the Drupal community, we already have quite a bit of our interface translated. As more translations are contributed to `localize.drupal.org`, we can get these updates easily using the Localization Update module. What about strings that haven't been translated yet? Well, how about translating those ourselves?

1. Let's start by doing this manually at the **Configuration | Regional and language | Translate interface | Translate** page. There is a string translation form provided where we can search for untranslated text in our site. If you restrict the search to untranslated strings in English, the search results will show all interface strings that need translation.

2. If you know what text you want to translate, then type some of the text into the **String contains** box and click on the **Filter** button. Note that the search text is case sensitive. In my case, I have the Meta Tags module installed, so I can search for `Add a meta tag`. If you don't have Meta Tags installed, try a different text string like `Add` or `Configure` or `help`.

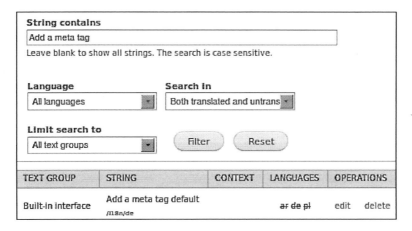

3. To translate one of the strings, click on the **edit** link and fill out the translation form. Since I don't speak any of my new site languages, I will use Google Translate (`translate.google.com`) to get the text. This is definitely not recommended for a real site but will suffice for our demo.

4. If you search again for your text in the translated strings, you will see that it is marked as translated for the languages where you provided the text.

So now you probably understand how you would change an existing translation. Simply find the text you want to modify, click on the **edit** link and change the strings as desired. This is a straightforward process, but navigating through the long list of strings on the **Translate** page is cumbersome. Also, we may only want to worry about text that we see directly on our site and translate as needed. To make this process easier, we will need another handy module, that is Localization Client (`drupal.org/project/l10n_client`).

1. Install the Localization Client module and flush your cache.
2. Now if you switch to another language, you will see a new toolbar at the bottom of the page.
3. Click on **TRANSLATE TEXT** on the bottom right and a useful form opens.

The actual link text depends on the translation available for **TRANSLATE TEXT** in the language you are working with.

The left side of the form shows all the text accessible from the current page. If the text is highlighted in green, there is a translation available and the translated text is shown. If there is no translation, then the text is in its source language, ready for you to translate.

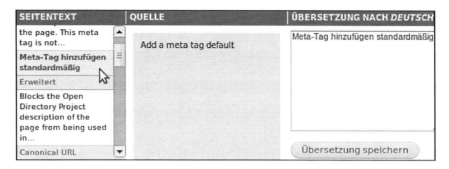

4. Click on the text and it will show up in the center column (marked **QUELLE** in the previous screenshot because "quelle" means "source" in German).

5. Then put the translated text into the box on the right and click on the **Save translation** button. If you want to use the source string as a template, click on the **Copy source** button first and then make your changes.

 The actual button text depends on the translations available for **Save translation** and **Copy source** in the language you are working with.

It is important to note that you might encounter strings such as the following:

```
Use the @vocab_name terms of the page being shown.
```

Take notice of the special use of the @ symbol, which indicates a string placeholder. For this example, @vocab_name is a placeholder that should remain unaltered because it will be filled in dynamically by the system. String placeholders can start with @, !, or %. The following is an example using all three:

```
Date & time (!date %time) can be changed on the
  <a href="@url">regional settings configuration page</a>.
```

Be careful to preserve these placeholders when you perform translations. The previous example in German might look similar to the following :

```
Datum & Uhrzeit (!date %time) finden Sie auf der
  <a href="@url">regionalen Einstellungen Konfiguration
  Seite geändert werden</a>.
```

Contributing translations back to the community

Now you know how to add and change translated UI text on your site. If you want to contribute your translations to the Drupal community, it's easy to do. Please do this if your translations are accurate! It benefits everyone using that language:

1. If you are willing to share your translations, install the Localization Client module and enable the sharing option at the **Configuration | Regional and language | Languages | Sharing** page:

2. Next, figure out which roles will be translating content. If there will be more than one translator, you'll probably want to add a dedicated translator role.

3. Update your permissions so the appropriate roles have the **Submit translations to localization server** permission enabled.

4. Flush your cache and switch to a user with this role.

5. After you have logged in as a user who can share translations, edit the user's profile page.

6. If you scroll down the page, you will have a new **Localization Client** section.

7. Follow the instructions for getting **Your Localization Server API key**.

Create a key on a real site for real translations and not for testing.

Your Localization Server API key

This is a unique key that will allow you to send translations /7216e1de332085bb1b63f9580c45428f₂.

8. Save your key and translate away! Your translations are very welcome. You can even update your drupal.org profile to show off your new contributions:

 I contributed Drupal translations

Translating English strings

One thing that you might want to do is change some of your English interface strings in some way. For example, maybe you want the lofty word "Taxonomy" changed to "Categories" as well as any related text.

You can find all the strings with "Taxonomy" in them by using the **Translate interface** form at **Configuration | Regional and language | Translation interface | Translate**. Make sure to search for both uppercase and lowercase strings.

Once you have the strings to change, you need a way to change them since this unfortunately can't be done out-of-the-box for English strings. I'll cover three options, namely modifying the settings.php file, using the String Overrides module, and creating a custom English language.

Flush your caches after trying any of these methods so the new text shows up.

Modifying the settings.php file

If you have a small number of strings to modify, then a quick way to change the strings is to put them in an array in your `settings.php` file as follows:

```
$conf['locale_custom_strings_en'][''] = array(
  'Taxonomy' => 'Categories',
  'Taxonomy term' => 'Category term',
);
```

Using the String Overrides module

Another option when working with a minimal number of strings is to use the String Overrides module. Just install the module (`drupal.org/project/stringoverrides`) and navigate to the config page at **Configuration | Regional and language | String overrides**. Then fill in the original text on the left and the replacement text on the right and click on **Save configuration**. Super easy!

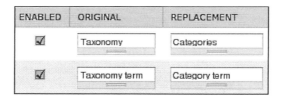

ENABLED	ORIGINAL	REPLACEMENT
☑	Taxonomy	Categories
☑	Taxonomy term	Category term

Creating a custom English language

If you plan on changing a lot of English strings, you can create a custom English language to replace your English language. If English is your default language, you can make the custom English language your default instead and then disable English. Then, if you are using the Localization Client or the Translate Interface page, you will be able to modify any of the English interface strings easily for your custom English language.

One problem with this approach is that it is not recommended that you change your default language once you have started translating content. Thus, a custom English language should only be added at the beginning of a project or, at least, before the localization process has begun or else the results might be bad.

For example, if you already have content in English and then create a new custom English, you'll end up with some nodes with the original English language code and some nodes with the new custom English language code (unless, of course, you go back and update all the old English content). Tread carefully or things can get confusing.

Reusing custom translated strings

If you want to reuse your translated strings for other websites, you can export the strings at **Configuration | Regional and language | Translate interface | Export**. Just choose the type of strings to export and click on the **Export** button and you'll get a .po file to save. Then you can import that .po file into your other Drupal websites via the **Configuration | Regional and language | Translate interface | Import** page. Neat!

General system configuration

We've made good progress by configuring our languages and translating our Drupal interface. You are probably anxious to start translating your content, but there are a few loose ends we should tie up first.

In this section, we'll configure some general system settings by updating the default country, time zone, and date/time formats. We will then work with the Variable Translation module to translate site information such as the site name and slogan. The section concludes with creating contact forms for our new languages.

Updating regional settings

Navigate to the **Configuration | Regional and language | Regional settings** page. You can choose your site's default country and first day of the week in the **Locale** settings.

In the time zones section, you can set the **Default time zone** as well as configure additional settings for your users. It's recommended that you allow users to set their own time zone, but the other settings can be chosen based on preference:

Default time zone

America/Los Angeles: Thursday, February 23, 2012 - 15:56 -0800

☑ Users may set their own time zone.

☐ Remind users at login if their time zone is not set.
Only applied if users may set their own time zone.

Time zone for new users

◉ Default time zone.

○ Empty time zone.

○ Users may set their own time zone at registration.

Only applied if users may set their own time zone.

Date and time formats

We can change the date and time settings for each language. First go to the **Configuration | Regional and language | Date and time** page and click on the **Localize** tab. Then click on the **edit** link for a language, and adjust your formats as desired:

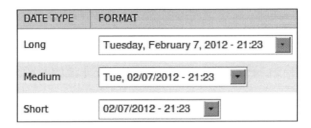

DATE TYPE	FORMAT
Long	Tuesday, February 7, 2012 - 21:23
Medium	Tue, 02/07/2012 - 21:23
Short	02/07/2012 - 21:23

Translating site variables

Drupal allows modules and themes to save data in a global variable table. This is useful for saving permanent information without having to create custom database tables. Some of the data in the variable table includes text strings that will be shown to users.

For example, the site name and slogan are variables that might show up at the top of the website depending on your theme. We want to be able to translate these strings for our languages.

Follow the given steps to translate your variables:

1. Install the Variable Translation module from the Internationalization package (`drupal.org/project/i18n`) and the Variable module (`drupal.org/project/variable`). If you only choose Variable Translation for installation, Drupal will show you what other modules need to be enabled due to dependencies. In this case, you will need the Internationalization, Variable, Variable Store, and Variable Realm modules.

2. After installing these modules, you will have another configuration area under your **Configuration | Regional and language** page called **Multilingual settings**.

> Regional settings
> Date and time
> Languages
> Translate interface
> Multilingual settings

3. Now navigate to **Configuration | Regional and language | Multilingual settings | Variables** and you will see a list of variables you can translate.

4. For now, enable the **Site name** and **Site slogan** checkboxes and click on **Save configuration**.

5. We will update the site name and slogan by going to the **Configuration | System | Site information** page. In English, my variables will look as shown in the following screenshot:

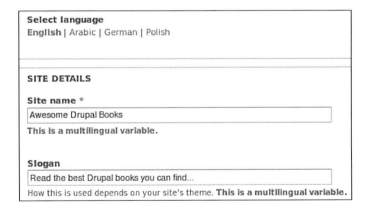

6. To translate these strings into German, click on the German **Select language** link at the top of the page. All the variables chosen for translation are marked with **This is a multilingual variable** underneath the field.

7. Fill the translated text into the form and save. Now when switching to German, the top of the page looks similar to the following screenshot:

8. Besides the variables we have translated, there are many others that you might want to translate as well, such as site e-mail messages. Note that as you add more modules, the list of variables may increase, so don't forget to come back to the Variable Translation configuration page as needed.

Customizing the contact form

We've done a lot in this chapter, but we have one more hurdle before moving on to our content. It is time to translate our site contact form.

1. Go ahead and enable the core Contact module and install the Contact Translation module from the Internationalization package (`drupal.org/project/i18n`).

   My English contact form is at `example.com/contact` and my German one is at `example.com/de/contact`. These already have translated text thanks to our interface translations. But there are a few more steps you need to do to finish the job.

2. Navigate to the **Structure | Contact form** config page. The default contact form is already set up.

CATEGORY	RECIPIENTS	SELECTED	OPERATIONS	
Website feedback	i18n@example.com	Yes	Edit	Delete

3. Click on the **Edit** link and you'll see the contact category settings. You can change the category name, recipients of the submissions, and auto-reply text.

4. Fill in your English auto-reply text and then click on **Save and translate**.

5. Your data will be saved and then you'll end up on the **Translate** tab.

LANGUAGE	TITLE	STATUS	OPERATIONS
English (source)	Website feedback	original	edit
Arabic	Website feedback	not translated	translate
German	Website feedback	not translated	translate
Polish	Website feedback	not translated	translate

6. If you click on the German **translate** link, the category name and auto-reply text will be pre-populated with the English values.

7. Just fill in the translation and click on **Save translation**:

Now if someone uses the German contact form, they will get an e-mail reply in German!

Summary

Whew! I don't know about you, but I'm tired. We did a lot in this chapter, so give yourself a pat on the back that you've made it this far. Let's do a quick review of all the good stuff we learned.

After we created our test website, we worked with languages. We added several new languages and then configured the detection settings to handle different URLs per language based on the language's path prefix. Then, we added a handy block for switching between each language with ease.

Once the languages were in place, we moved on to Drupal interface translation. We got translation files directly from `localize.drupal.org` and imported them into our site. To make the job easier, we installed the Localization Update module to get the translation files for us automatically. We then learned that, unfortunately, not all the UI text has been translated. So we added our own string translations that can be shared back with the community. This process was simplified with the Localization Client module. For the last part of the UI translation section, we learned different methods for translating English strings and how to export our string translations for use on other Drupal websites.

We finished the chapter with a grab bag of configuration settings. We updated the default country and time zone in the regional settings and the date/time formats for each language. In the end, we translated a couple of site variables including the site name and updated the contact form settings for our languages.

Now let's move on to translating our content!

Working with Content

In the previous chapter, we set up a test site, translated our interface, and configured general system settings to support multiple languages. Now we will start our content translation process!

The first part of this chapter focuses on nodes. We'll work with the node translation method which creates multiple nodes, and the field translation method that uses one multilingual node. We will look at examples and use cases for both methods.

After our nodes are translated, we'll configure non-node core entities (comments, users, and taxonomy terms) using field translation. The chapter concludes with a quick look at built-in Drupal content pages, namely the default home page, taxonomy term pages, and search.

Nodes

For the majority of Drupal websites, most content exists in nodes. These nodes come in different shapes and sizes as defined by a node's content type. The information, if any, that needs translating for a particular node depends on how the content is used, so there is no cookie-cutter formula for creating multilingual nodes. You will need to decide how to deal with translation for each and every content type. In this section, we will go over the different approaches for multilingual node content. We will work with concrete examples to help you figure out the methods to implement on your own site.

Enabling multilingual support

For the exercises, it's useful to have a few content types to work with. If you are using the demo website, you have several to choose from including **Article**, **Blog entry**, **Basic page**, and **Drupal Book**.

The first three are pretty self-explanatory. **Drupal Book** is a custom content type for displaying a particular Drupal book title. For simplicity, **Drupal Book** nodes are not configured for e-commerce, but check out `kristen.org/drupal7-i18n-commerce` to learn about internationalization for the Drupal Commerce module.

To enable multilingual support on your site, follow these steps:

1. Choose a content type and go to its main config page (for example, for **Blog entry**, go to **Structure | Content types | Blog entry | Edit**).

2. Now click on the **Publishing options** tab towards the bottom of the form and you will see the following options since the Locale module is enabled:

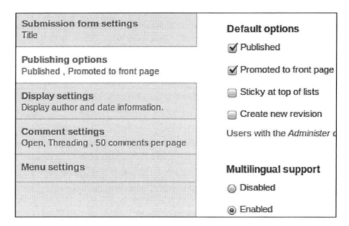

3. Choose the **Enabled** radio button in the **Multilingual support** section and then click on **Save content type**. Now any node of this content type can have a language associated with it. If I edit a **Blog entry** node, I now have a **Language** field on my node edit form.

The **Language** drop-down includes all enabled site languages as well as a **Language neutral** option. Choose **Language neutral** if you have language-independent content. For example, if you have an **Image** content type with an **image** field in it, then an **Image** node might not have linguistic content and could be set as **Language neutral**.

Node translation model

In previous versions of Drupal, content translation was done by copying the source node for each language. The source node and its associated translated nodes together form a translation set such as the grouped nodes shown in the following figure:

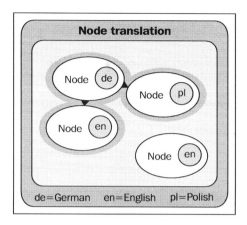

The node translation model is still available for Drupal 7. Note that for Drupal 8, the current plan is to combine the node translation model and field translation model, discussed later in this chapter, to unify the architecture.

Node translation might be useful when your content will be mostly or fully translated. For example, if you have a blog post or an article, it is likely that you'll want to translate everything in the text except perhaps meta information such as the author's name and the date of the post. There might be common fields that the nodes should "share" such as an image or a video, but those shared fields can be handled with some configuration.

Another good reason to use node translation is if you want to track each node separately, for example, if you want users to vote on different translations of an article, or if you want them to flag translated blog posts, for instance, "I like this!" or "Bad translation!" You might even want a different workflow for each node to allow published nodes and unpublished nodes within the same translation set.

Conversely, you should now have a better idea of when you don't want to use the node translation model. Typically this is the case if you have a minimal number of fields that need translating or if you want to make sure to track the node as one object for whatever purpose (voting, flagging, workflow, tracking, and so on). For these use cases, we will look at some examples in the field translation section later in this chapter.

Configuring node translation

We need to configure a few different things to get our node translation set up. In this section, we'll enable the required modules, configure our content types, and change some node display options. Oh, and we'll translate content too!

Content type settings

Let's start with configuring our content type by following these steps:

1. Enable the core Content Translation module.

2. If we go back to our content type configuration page (for example, for Blog entry, go to **Structure | Content types | Blog entry | Edit**) and click on the **Publishing options** tab, we have a new **Multilingual support** option:

3. Select the **Enabled, with translation** radio button and click on **Save content type**.

4. Now if you view a node page for that content type, you'll see a new handy **Translate** tab:

 If you don't see a **Translate** tab, then most likely you have that node's language set as **Language neutral**. Edit the node, choose a language, and save it, so that the **Translate** tab will appear.

5. Click on the **Translate** tab and you will be shown a summary of the current translations for that node.

LANGUAGE	TITLE	STATUS	OPERATIONS
English (source)	Multilingual Drupal rocks!	Published	edit
Arabic	n/a	Not translated	add translation
German	n/a	Not translated	add translation
Polish	n/a	Not translated	add translation

6. To translate the node, click on **add translation** for a particular language.

Since we already configured the interface in *Chapter 2, Setting up the Basics: Languages, UI Translation, and System Settings*, we will see the translated UI strings on the node edit page. For example, I see the German Drupal interface when adding a translation for German:

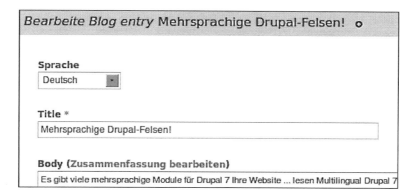

Node display options

By default, translation links are added to the node links for any available translations (for example, **English** in the following screenshot):

The decision to show translation links on teasers and node view pages is a matter of preference. These links can improve usability if you have a small number of languages, but the UI can look ugly if you have too many.

To turn translation links off completely, follow these steps:

1. Install the Multilingual Content module from the Internationalization package (`drupal.org/project/i18n`).

2. Flush the cache and go to **Configuration | Regional and language | Multilingual settings | Node options**.

3. Select **Hide content translation links** and click on **Save configuration**.

4. On this page, you can disable the **Switch interface for translating** option if desired. You can also set the default language for content types that have multilingual support disabled. This can be set to **The site's default language** or to **Language neutral** depending on the type of content you expect to store:

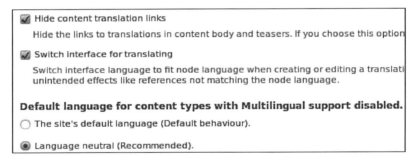

The Multilingual Content module from the Internationalization package adds a **Language** field to the content types. Typically you won't want this **Language** field shown when viewing a node. It can be hidden by performing the following steps:

1. Go to the content type's **Manage display** page (for example, for the **Blog entry** content type, this is at **Structure | Content types | Blog entry | Manage display**).

2. Choose **Hidden** for the **Language** field.

3. Click on **Save**.

4. Click on the small **Teaser** sub-tab and repeat.

New and existing translations

Now you can go back and create more translations using the same process:

1. View the node page and click on the **Edit** tab.
2. Choose language and click on the **Save** button.
3. Click on the **Translate** tab.
4. Click on the **add translation** link, translate the content, and click on **Save**.

If you have an existing German node which should be the translation of an existing English node, then clicking on the **add translation** link won't help you because both nodes already exist. How do we link these nodes together in a translation set? Fortunately the Internationalization package comes to the rescue again:

1. Click on the **Translate** tab and you'll see a useful form at the bottom of the page since the Multilingual Content module is installed.
2. To use an existing node, just type the node title into the auto-complete text field to find it.
3. Don't forget to click on **Update translations** after you find the right nodes!

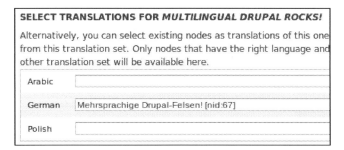

Synchronizing shared fields

There are times when a content field is not dependent on language and doesn't need translating. For example, an image might be language-independent and could be used for all nodes in a translation set. The simplest way to deal with these types of fields is to use the Synchronize Translations module which is part of the Internationalization package.

1. Install the Synchronize Translations module (`drupal.org/project/i18n`) and then navigate back to your content type configuration page. In my case, I'll go to the **Article** content type at **Structure | Content types | Article | Edit**.

2. You will now see a **Synchronize translations** tab at the bottom of the form.

3. Click on the **Synchronize translations** tab.

4. Choose the fields you want to keep in sync.

5. Click on **Save content type**.

 Be very careful when choosing the fields you want to synchronize. For example, it is highly unlikely you will want to select the **Body** field. Say you do select it and create an English node with body text. If you then translate the node for German and change the body text, the original English body text would be wiped out and replaced with the one you provided for the German node. This is probably not what you want to happen!

For this example, I edited the **Article** content type and chose a number of fields to be in sync, including a custom **Image** field. Now when I edit any **Article** nodes, the image will be shared across all nodes in a translation set. Try it for yourself!

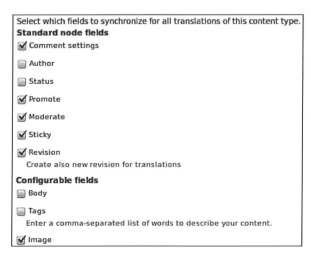

Extra content type options

The Internationalization module package is a treasure-trove of useful goodies. To see a few more settings from the Multilingual Content module, navigate to your content type configuration page (for example, **Structure | Content types | Article | Edit**). Then click on the **Multilingual settings** tab to see some new options.

These are the extended language options:

- **Set current language as default for new content**: This is a good option to enable for all multilingual content types. If enabled and you are navigating the site in Polish, then Polish will be auto-selected for your node's language when creating content.

- **Require language (Do not allow Language Neutral)**: This one is pretty self-explanatory. When you create a node, the **Language neutral** option will not be available in the **Language** drop-down list. Therefore you'll need to choose a specific language. This option is good for any content types that must be translated.

- **Lock language (Cannot be changed)**: If you enable this setting, then the node's language cannot be changed after the node is created. This option might be useful if you are setting your language correctly each and every time, but it will end up being a pain if you don't!

Here are some options for extended language support:

- **Normal**: When you edit content, only the site's enabled languages will be available in the **Language** field. Most sites should stick with this setting.

- **Extended**: All of the defined languages will be listed in the **Language** drop-down whether enabled or not. This option is useful when you want some languages for the UI but need more languages for the content. For example, you should use this option if you are staging content for a language that shouldn't be made public yet.

- **Extended, but not displayed**: Same as the **Extended** option, but translation links will not be shown for disabled languages.

Field translation model

In the previous sections, we explored why we might use the node translation model for certain content types. When that method is not appropriate, we can use field translation instead. The field translation model uses one node rather than a set of nodes where individual fields are translated as needed, as illustrated next for the **Title** and **Body** fields.

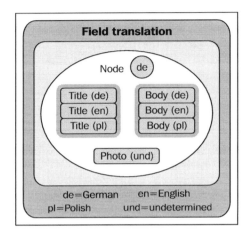

Entity fields were introduced in Drupal 7, so field translation is not available in earlier versions of Drupal. As mentioned previously, the Drupal 8 Multilingual Initiative is investigating how to combine the node and field translation models together for Drupal 8.

Field translation is useful when you have a minimal number of content fields to translate or when you need to maintain one multilingual node. For example, a product content type typically has fields such as price, images, and manufacturer that probably should not be translated. For a product node, translatable information would likely include title, body, and similar descriptive text, so those specific fields should be configured for translation.

A product content type is a good candidate for the field translation method for other reasons as well. When someone buys a product, it is tracked. For example, we can find out how many people bought the product. If we use node translation for products, then our tracking is per node. We wouldn't know how many people bought a particular product, but instead would have the total for the number of people who bought the product using the German interface, the French interface, and so on. This isn't usually what we want.

Other examples of when field translation makes sense include events and organic groups. When someone signs up for an event, it is important to track the event data in one node. For organic groups, the main group node is the key to membership, so it would be problematic to have multiple nodes. Field translation is the best solution when you have these types of language-unaware node relationships.

Configuring field translation

As with node translation, we need to configure several things before we start using field translation. In this section, we will enable the necessary modules, configure our entity and content type settings, and then translate our content.

Entity settings

To configure your entity settings, follow these steps:

1. Install the Entity Translation module (`drupal.org/project/ entity_translation`).

2. Entity Translation adds a new **Content language detection** section at **Configuration | Regional and language | Languages | Detection and selection**. Navigate to that page and update the settings so that the **Content language detection** section matches the **User interface text language detection** section (rearrange the items as needed and make sure the same items are checked or unchecked).

3. Enable the **Interface** method and move it to the top. This option will try to use the interface detection settings when possible, but it isn't always reliable. This is why you should match the interface detection section options as well.

4. Click on **Save settings** when you're done.

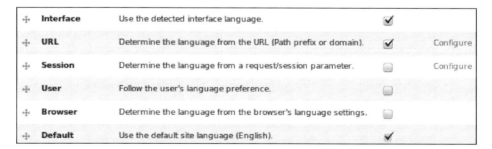

5. Now you need to replace your current language switcher block called **Language switcher (User interface text)** with the new **Language switcher (Content)** block. If you don't change the block, the switcher links won't be correct.

6. To enable your nodes for translation, you now have a new Entity Translation config page at **Configuration | Regional and language | Entity translation**.

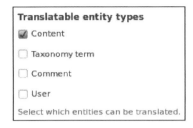

We can stick with the default entity settings since we are focusing on node content at the moment. We'll look at the other entity options later in this chapter.

Content type settings

When configuring our content type settings, we will need to choose a content type for field translation and then proceed with the following steps:

1. Go to your content type config page (for example, edit **Drupal Book** at **Structure | Content types | Drupal Book | Edit**), click on the **Publishing options** tab, and you'll see a new option for **Multilingual support**:

2. Choose **Enabled, with field translation** and click on **Save content type**. Note that for earlier module versions, the option is **Enabled, with entity translation**. Now we need to decide which fields to translate. **Drupal Book** has a number of fields including **Title**, **Image**, **Description** (Body), and **Drupal Version**:

LABEL	NAME	FIELD
Title	title_field	Text
Image	field_image	Image
Description	body	Long text and summary
Drupal Version	field_drupal_version	Term reference

An interesting thing about the **Title** field in Drupal 7 is that it's technically not a real "field" (it is considered a "property"). This is a problem when using field translation because we want to translate the node's **Title**.

3. The workaround is to install the Title module (`drupal.org/project/title`) and the Entity API module (`drupal.org/project/entity`). Install both of those now and then go to the content type's **Manage fields** page.

4. You'll see a **replace** link for the **Title**. Click on **replace**, select the **Replace title with a field instance** checkbox, and click on **Save settings**:

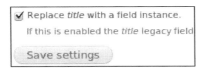

The Title module will do some magic and then the **Title** will be transformed into a bona fide **Text** field. One oddity is that the new **Title** field will show up on the node view page (you'll have two titles!), so it needs to be hidden.

5. Go to the **Manage display** page for your content type, choose **<Hidden>** for the **Title**, and click on **Save**:

For **Drupal Book**, let's configure the **Description** (Body), so it can be translated. The Title module will enable translation for the **Title** field for us.

6. Go back to the **Manage fields** page.

7. Click on **edit** for the **Description** (Body) field and the bottom of the form will look similar to the next screenshot. Note that it will say **BODY FIELD SETTINGS** when editing a **Body** field that has not been renamed.

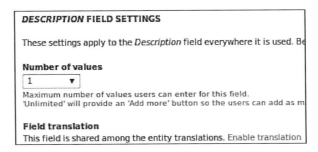

8. If you don't have content yet, there will be a **Users may translate this field** checkbox, otherwise, there will be an **Enable translation** link. Select the checkbox and save the settings, or click on the link. If there is content, a **Disable translation** link will be available if you need to turn off translation.

9. Repeat this process for all fields you want to translate.

 Author and status are not "fields" and cannot be translated using field translation. If you need a different author or workflow per translation, you'll need to use node translation and the Synchronize Translations module similar to what we did earlier in this chapter.

Translating content

Now that the fields have been configured, we can translate our content. Edit an existing node or create a new one, set its language to the default language, and save the node. The **Translate** tab will be available just as it was when we used the node translation model.

Click on **Translate** and the UI will look familiar. To add translations, just follow the same process as before:

1. Click on the **add translation** link.

2. Translate content and click on the **Save** button.

3. Repeat for each language.

Using the language switcher

Because of the way field translation works, notice that all languages are "available" in the language switcher for our node even when translations are actually missing. These duplicate pages affect the site's SEO, which will be discussed in *Chapter 5, Panels, SEO, and More!*.

Another thing to remember is that, for field translation, we are using one node. So, if you click on any language in the language switcher and edit the node, you are actually editing the same node, no matter what the interface language is. This is very important to keep in mind, particularly if you are using both node translation and field translation models. It can become confusing at times if you aren't paying attention. Let's recap:

- When you use the language switcher for node translation, you will be viewing a different node. In that case, if you edit the node, you'll see the node edit page for the translated content. Saving the node will affect the translated node and not the source node (except for synchronized fields). Translated content can be handled with this method or via the **Translate** tab process.

- When you use the language switcher for field translation, you will be viewing the same node but the translated fields will show up to match your chosen language. If you edit the node, you'll see the node edit page for the source node content (the only node). To translate content, you must click on the **Translate** tab and use that process.

 At the time of writing, there is an open Entity Translation issue to allow field translation via the node edit page (drupal.org/node/1282018).

Non-node entities

Although translating nodes is usually the bulk of the content translation burden, there might be "content" from other entities as well. This section walks us through the configuration for these non-node core entities, namely, comments, users, and taxonomy terms.

Comments

For each content type, you will need to decide if it makes sense to translate comments. If comments are coming from the general public, then it's unlikely that they should be translated. But, if there are comments that you control, then translating them might make sense. For example, if you have a company blog where only employees make comments and the blog posts will be translated, you might decide to translate the comments as well.

Unlike nodes, comments can only be handled using field translation as follows:

1. Navigate to **Configuration | Regional and language | Entity translation**.

2. Select the **Comment** checkbox and click on **Save configuration**.

3. Now we can enable field translation for any of our comment fields. To do this, we need to choose a content type, so we can get to the correct configuration page. I'll start with the **Blog entry** content type at **Structure | Content types | Blog entry | Edit**.

4. Navigate to your content type config page and then click on the **Comment fields** tab.

   Since the Title module is installed, we have a **replace** link available for the **Subject** field.

5. Click on **replace**.

6. Select the **Replace subject with a field instance** checkbox.

7. Click **Save settings**. Your comment fields should look similar to the following screenshot:

Author	author	Author textfield
Subject	subject_field	Text
Comment	comment_body	Long text

You now need to hide the new **Subject** field from the display, so that you don't have two subject lines showing up in the comments:

1. Click on the **Comment display** tab.

2. Choose **<Hidden>** for the **Subject**.

3. Click on **Save**.

 You need to repeat the **Subject** field replacement process for all content type comment entities that will be translated.

Translation for the **Subject** field is enabled by the Title module, so you just need to configure the **Comment** field using the following steps:

1. Go back to the **Comment fields** tab.

2. Click on the **Comment** field's **edit** link and scroll down the form. Click on the **Enable translation** link if you have existing content (otherwise, check the **Users may translate this field** checkbox and save the settings).

3. Edit a node comment (or add a new one and save it) and you will see a **Translate** tab.

4. Click on the **Translate** tab and you will find a familiar translation overview page:

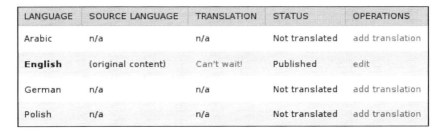

LANGUAGE	SOURCE LANGUAGE	TRANSLATION	STATUS	OPERATIONS
Arabic	n/a	n/a	Not translated	add translation
English	(original content)	Can't wait!	Published	edit
German	n/a	n/a	Not translated	add translation
Polish	n/a	n/a	Not translated	add translation

5. The process for translating comments is the same as the process for translating nodes. Click on the **add translation** link, translate the content, and click on **Save translation**. Repeat for each language.

Language assignment

When creating a comment, the language assigned is based on the interface language. If I'm viewing the site in German and create a comment, then the language for the comment will be German as well. This is true whether the node being commented on was translated using node translation or field translation.

Comment display

When viewing comments on nodes that use node translation, you will see only the comments associated with the particular node. If there is an English node and an associated German node, then you will see different comments for each since the comments are not shared.

For field-translated nodes this is different since there is only one node. By default, you see all comments, and comments show up in the selected language when possible. For example, if you are viewing German content, a comment will show up in German if there is a German translation or the comment's source language is German. If German is not available, the source comment will be shown (in whatever language). If you prefer that only comments with the selected language be displayed, then follow the given steps:

1. Edit the content type for the comments (for example, **Structure | Content types | Blog entry | Edit**).
2. Click on the **Comment settings** tab.
3. Select the **Filter comments per language** checkbox.
4. Click on **Save content type**.

Users

Although it is a bit strange to think of users as content, users can have fields just like nodes and comments. So, just like for node and comment fields, we can enable translation for any of the user fields. When might this make sense? For general users, it probably doesn't. But, if your site showcases your employees, you might want to translate profile information for your employee users.

1. First, enable field translation for users by going to **Configuration | Regional and language | Entity translation**.
2. Select **User** and click on **Save configuration**.
3. Now navigate to **Configuration | People | Account settings | Manage fields** and you'll see the default user fields, namely **User name and password** and **Timezone**. These aren't actually real "fields" (they are usually referred to as "properties"), so we can't enable translation for any of them.
4. Add a new **Long text** field called **Bio**.
5. Enable the **Users may translate this field** checkbox when saving the field settings. This new **Bio** field is now translatable.
6. Create a new user or edit an existing one and fill in the **Bio** text.

7. Now when you view a user, you will see a **Translate** tab. Click on the tab to get to the translation overview page:

LANGUAGE	SOURCE LANGUAGE	TRANSLATION	STATUS	OPERATIONS
Arabic	n/a	n/a	Not translated	add translation
English	(original content)	view	Published	edit
German	n/a	n/a	Not translated	add translation
Polish	n/a	n/a	Not translated	add translation

Translating user information follows familiar steps:

1. Click on the **add translation** link.
2. Translate content and click on the **Save translation** button.
3. Repeat for all languages.

Taxonomy terms

Taxonomy terms can be associated with nodes (or other entities) by using a **Term reference** field. For example, the demo site has a **Blog entry** content type with a **Blog Tags** term reference field.

One way to deal with different translations having different taxonomy terms is to configure the term reference field itself to be translatable. When using node translation, this will be the default behavior unless the field is configured with the Synchronize Translations module as discussed previously.

For nodes using field translation, use the process explained earlier for content type fields. This approach makes the most sense when you are using completely different and unrelated terms for each translation.

The other approach, which is more typical, is to configure the taxonomy term entities. One complication is that we have different ways to handle this configuration.

First, we can use the field translation method for term fields similar to what we did for node, comment, and user fields. Second, the Internationalization package provides a flexible Taxonomy Translation module for translating vocabularies and terms in a variety of ways.

Field translation will be addressed here but the Taxonomy Translation module will be covered in *Chapter 4, Configuring Blocks, Menus, Taxonomy, and Views*, since it is a very different approach. These two methods can be used in parallel (for different vocabularies).

Field translation is useful when you have custom fields for your taxonomy terms because the Taxonomy Translation module only handles the term name and description. For example, if you have a "**Slang**" vocabulary and decide to add an "**Example Usage**" field, then it would make sense to use field translation, so that all term fields (**Name**, **Description**, **Example Usage**, and so on) are translatable.

Another reason you might choose field translation instead of taxonomy translation is just for simplicity (there are fewer modules to deal with).

Configuring field translation for the taxonomy term entities is similar to what we did for nodes, comments, and users:

1. First, enable the **Taxonomy term** entity type at **Configuration | Regional and language | Entity translation** and save the settings.
2. Now you need to choose a vocabulary and navigate to its **Manage fields** page (for example, **Structure | Taxonomy | Tags | Manage fields**).
3. You will see **replace** links for both the **Name** and **Description** fields because the Title module is installed.
4. Click on **replace** for the **Name** field, select the **Replace name with a field instance** checkbox, and click on **Save settings**.
5. Repeat this process for the **Description** field.

 If you have custom taxonomy term fields, you can enable translation for those, in the way the user **Bio** field was configured previously.

With field translation configured, you can now edit any of your terms in the vocabulary and find a **Translate** tab. On the **Translate** tab page, you'll see the translation overview where you can do the usual, that is, click on the **add translation** link, translate **Name** and **Description**, save the translation, and repeat for your languages.

Once the terms are translated, the way they are used depends on the content they are associated with. If the node's term reference field is shared for all node translations, then just choose your terms for one node translation and, when you view a different node translation, the translated terms will show up. If the node's term reference field is not shared, then just choose the correct language-specific terms when editing each translation.

Custom entities

Drupal core provides node, comment, user, and taxonomy term entities, but contributed modules can also define custom entities in their code. For example, the Commerce module defines entities for products, payments, and customers, and the Organic Groups module has entities for groups and memberships.

In theory, by using the Entity Translation module, you can configure field translation for any entity type with fields. The process would be similar to what we did previously. But, in practice, it might not work depending on the entity. For example, translating **Commerce Product** fields (from the Commerce module) does work (check out `kristen.org/drupal7-i18n-commerce` for a tutorial). For other custom entities, check the module's project page or issue queue to see if field translation is fully supported.

Node listing and search pages

As you have been clicking around your site, you might have noticed something odd. On pages with lists of content such as the default home page and taxonomy term pages, content is shown in all languages. In this section, we will fix this issue as well as look at language support for core search functionality.

Home page

If you are using the demo site or a site built from scratch, you start off with the default home page provided by Drupal (`/node`). To get the home page to show nodes based on language, install the Multilingual Select module from the Internationalization package (`drupal.org/project/i18n`). Now when you change languages, you'll only see language-neutral nodes and nodes in the chosen language. The module can be configured at **Configuration | Regional and language | Multilingual settings | Selection**.

At the time of writing, the Multilingual Select module doesn't handle nodes that have been translated using the field translation model (drupal.org/node/1398770).

It's unlikely you'll want to use the default home page for your real website. Instead, you might use a views page, a panels page, or something defined in custom code. We will discuss multilingual views pages in *Chapter 4*, *Configuring Blocks, Menus, Taxonomy, and Views*, and panels pages in *Chapter 5*, *Panels, SEO, and More!*. If you are writing a custom module to generate your home page, check out *Chapter 5* for more details on module development for a multilingual website. *Chapter 5* also covers handling a separate home page per language which improves SEO.

Taxonomy term pages

Drupal automatically provides taxonomy pages for each term in every vocabulary on your site. By default, node terms show up on node view pages and each term is linked to its taxonomy page. With the Multilingual Select module enabled, these taxonomy pages will only show nodes that are language-neutral or match the selected language. You can use the language switcher to switch between taxonomy term pages for each language.

Search

If you are using the built-in Drupal search, users with **Use advanced search** permission can search for node and comment content based on language. The core user search does not have any advanced search functionality. If you need more sophisticated search features with multilingual support, check out the Apache Solr Search Integration module.

 For nodes using field translation, at the time of writing, content is only searchable using keywords in the default language. Track the issue at drupal.org/node/1291388. There is a contributed module, Search API Entity Translation, in development that might help in the interim.

Summary

Wow! I'm sure you'll agree that we just covered a lot of material. Configuring a multilingual website is not for the faint of heart! Let's quickly recap the important items we covered in this chapter.

We first focused on the node translation method using the core Content Translation module. Example content types were discussed to better understand when node translation works best. We then configured content types, display options, and extended features from the Internationalization package, and actually translated some nodes!

After node translation, we moved on to the field translation model. More examples were reviewed to help us know when to choose field translation over node translation. Then the Entity Translation module was installed and we configured entity and content type settings. With the configuration in place, we translated some content via fields, and then discussed the differences between the two translation processes and possible gotchas.

With nodes completed, we took a look at non-node core entities (comments, users, and taxonomy terms) which were configured using the field translation process. Then, custom entities were addressed briefly.

Finally, the built-in Drupal content pages were explored including the default home page, taxonomy term pages, and search. We turned on the Multilingual Select module to add multilingual support to the home page and taxonomy term pages. Then we finished up by taking a look at the default language support for the core search feature.

We're on the home stretch. Let's move on to blocks, menus, taxonomy, and views!

4
Configuring Blocks, Menus, Taxonomy, and Views

In the previous chapter, we translated content and looked at core content pages. In this chapter, we'll discuss the standard components of a Drupal site, namely, blocks, menus, taxonomy, and views.

First, we'll start by configuring language-specific and multilingual blocks and menus. Then, taxonomy terms will be revisited using different multilingual options provided by the Taxonomy Translation module. The chapter concludes with creating language-aware views for nodes, comments, taxonomy terms, and users.

Blocks

Modules can provide blocks, or we can create simple ones ourselves. A block should be configured appropriately based on its content. We might have a block that is language-independent such as an image. Some blocks might only make sense for one language, for example an advertisement targeted at German users. Other block content, such as footer text or instructions, might be relevant for some or all languages. In this section, we'll configure blocks for different use cases including a block created by a module.

Language-specific blocks

For language-independent blocks, you don't need to do anything special. Just create your blocks as usual. But, if you have blocks that need to only show up for certain languages, you'll need the Block Languages module.

1. Install the Block Languages module from the Internationalization package (`drupal.org/project/i18n`) and go to **Structure | Blocks | Add block**.

2. Let's create a block that will only be shown for one language. Fill in the **Block title**, **Block description**, and **Block body**, and then click on the **Languages** tab at the bottom of the form.

3. Now select a language and click on **Save block**:

4. Place the block where content with the chosen language is available. In my case, I'll create a block with German text and put it on my blog pages. This block will only show up if I'm viewing German blog content:

Translating blocks

When we add body text for a block, we can choose its text format (**Filtered HTML, Full HTML, Plain text**, and so on). So, before continuing with block translation, we need to make sure that we can translate strings that have been provided in different text formats.

1. Go to **Configuration | Regional and language | Multilingual settings | Strings**.

2. Select **Filtered HTML** and **Full HTML** in the **Translatable text formats** section (**Plain text** should already be selected) and click on **Save configuration**.

 Full HTML should only be used for trusted roles, and content gets translated prior to being filtered, so only use verified translations.

Now let's translate a block:

1. Edit a block (or create a new one), click on the **Languages** tab, and select **Make this block translatable**.

2. Do not choose a language in this case as we want this block shown for all languages:

 You can also create blocks for a subset of your languages. This can be combined with translation, so that a translated block is only available for some languages.

3. You'll now have a **Save and translate** button. So click on that and you'll see the translation overview page for the block.

4. Now you know what to do. Click on **translate**, translate content, click on **Save translation**, and repeat for all languages. Isn't consistency great?

Another nice feature is that we have a handy **Translate** link in the block's contextual links.

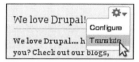

Once the translations are in place, the block content will match the interface language. For my example, I translated a custom "We love Drupal!" block to German and now it has the title "Wir lieben Drupal!" when viewing the German blog page:

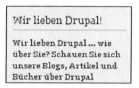

Blocks provided by modules

To handle a block provided by a module, our steps will be different because the text will be coming from the module code. Instead of using the **Translate** tab similar to what we used for custom blocks, we'll need to follow the string translation process used in *Chapter 2, Setting up the Basics: Languages, UI Translation, and System Settings*. Let's walk through this with an example by using the core **Powered by Drupal** block:

1. Go to **Structure | Blocks**, position the **Powered by Drupal** block in your footer region, and then configure the block to have a title (for example, "We are...").

2. Also, since we added a custom block title, click on the **Languages** tab, select **Make this block translatable**, and save the block.

 The usual **Translate** tab process lets us translate the block title if we override the title provided by the module, but it doesn't let us translate the block body text.

3. To translate the block title and body, go to **Configuration | Regional and language | Translate interface | Translate**.

4. Type in `Powered by` (case sensitive) in the **String contains** box and click on **Filter**. The `Powered by` text will show up as translated in the results since the translation is available (from our work in *Chapter 2, Setting up the Basics: Languages, UI Translation, and System Settings*).

 The default German translation is the same as the English text (`Powered by`).

TEXT GROUP	STRING	CONTEXT	LANGUAGES	OPERATIONS
Built-in interface	Powered by <a href="@poweredby">Drupal</a>		ar de pl	edit delete

5. Click on the **edit** link, add your translation, and click on **Save translations**.

6. Repeat the process for your custom block title text.

7. Flush all caches and take a look!

Our block will now have the new translated title and body text! For German, I changed "Powered by" to be the German translation of "Presented by," so it looks as follows:

Wir sind...

Präsentiert von Drupal

Menus

Menus are added to websites so that users can find content easily. We'll need to configure our site menus based on how they are used for each language. A menu might make sense for all languages because it links to language-independent content. Some menus might point to language-specific pages and should only be shown for the associated language. For other menus, the same navigation elements might be appropriate for some or all languages, so we'll need a multilingual menu.

Multilingual menus are not supported by Drupal core, so we will use the contributed Menu Translation module from the Internationalization package. But, before we try the different module options, the following figure provides examples of how we can handle menu items using Menu Translation. For language-independent menus, we can use the default option. For language-specific menus, we can use the **Fixed Language** option. For multilingual menus, we can use the **Translate and Localize** option (which has been split into two in the figure to illustrate the differences between "localize" and "translate").

In the figure, **NT** stands for "node-translated" and **FT** stands for "field-translated".

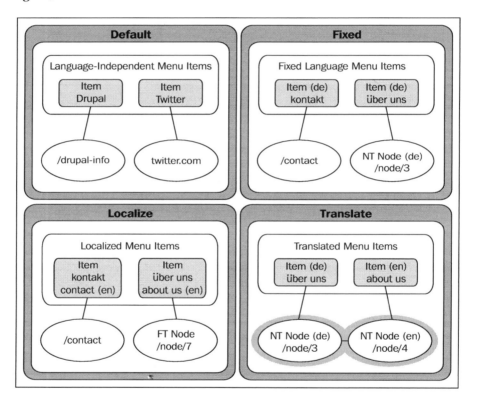

Language-specific menus

For language-independent menus, you don't need to do anything special. Just create the menu as usual. For language-specific menus, we'll need the Menu Translation module.

1. Install the Menu Translation module from the Internationalization package (`drupal.org/project/i18n`) and then create or edit your menu. For example, I'll edit a custom footer menu at **Structure | Menus | Footer menu | Edit**.

2. In the new **Translation mode** section, choose **Fixed Language** and a **Language** field will appear.

3. Select a language, click on **Save**, and add or update your menu items as needed.

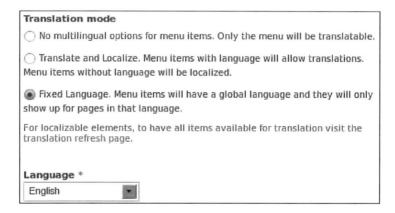

Now we need to see the menu somewhere, so let's configure the menu block.

4. Go to **Structure | Blocks**, position the menu block, and click on **Save blocks**.

5. Edit the block, select the language to match the menu, and save. This menu block will only be shown when viewing content in the matching language.

6. If desired, repeat the process so you have one menu block per language.

Multilingual menus

You can choose to make one menu per language but usually this is best when each menu is very different. When menus will be similar across languages, we can make a multilingual menu. A typical use case is the **Main menu** since it often makes sense to use the same global navigation regardless of language. For the demo site, the **Main menu** has links to common pages such as **About Us, News, Search, Contact Us**, and so on.

Let's create a multilingual menu:

1. First, add a menu or edit an existing one (for example, for the **Main menu**, go to **Structure | Menus | Main menu | Edit**), choose the **Translate and Localize** option, and save the menu.

2. To translate the menu's name, there is a **Translate** tab available when viewing the menu links or editing the menu. Just click on the tab and follow the regular translation process.

3. If necessary, position the menu block on the site as before.

Now that the menu has been configured, we can handle each menu item. Things can get a bit confusing at this point since the process will change depending on the type of menu item. A few different scenarios are explained in the next sections for better clarity.

Node pages

You would most likely want menu items that point directly to nodes. For example, on my demo site, the **About Us** link points to node/5 for English and that node can be translated. When using nodes translated via node translation, we can proceed as follows:

1. Add or edit a menu item for the source node (for example, **About Us** and node/5) and save the menu item. Note that the menu item's language will automatically be associated with the node's language. Now you have two ways of adding the translated nodes.

2. The first option is to edit the menu item again. Click on the **Translate** tab, and translate as usual while making sure to change the menu item's **Path** to point to the translated node page. After you click on **Save translation**, a new menu item and menu item translation set will be created for you.

3. Alternatively, add a new menu item directly for the translated node page and save. Then you can associate this menu item with the first one as follows:

    ○ Edit either menu item

    ○ Click on the **Translate** tab

    ○ Choose the correct mapping in the **Translations** section below the translation overview table

    ○ Click on **Save**

Now when you view the menu on the site and toggle between languages, the appropriate menu item title and node link will be displayed.

At the time of writing, field-translated nodes are not supported well in menus. There are some possible workarounds such as using the node/[nid]/view page or a fully-qualified URL (for example, http://example.com/node/[nid]) for the menu item path. But, these options end up with undesirable side effects including the active menu item not being set for the associated page. Since there are several related issues to solve, check the issue queues for both the Entity Translation and Internationalization modules to track progress.

Pages with the same link

For some pages, the same path should be used for all languages. For example, the demo site has a **Contact Us** menu item that links to /contact. In this case, we only need one menu item where the title and description are translated. This method is referred to as "localize" because there is only one menu item object.

1. Add or edit a menu item for a page where the same link should be used for all languages (for example, **Contact Us** and contact). Leave the language set to **Language neutral** and save the menu item. Note that the String Translation source language (that we set in *Chapter 2, Setting up the Basics: Languages, UI Translation, and System Settings*) will be used for the menu item even though it is set to **Language neutral** (yes, it is confusing).

2. Edit the menu item again, click on the **Translate** tab, and translate as usual.

Pages with different links

The last scenario we will cover is when a page has a different path per language. On the demo site, the **News** page is generated from a view and has the path /articles. We could create a different view page that was for German and uses the path /german-articles. Then we'd need to create two (related) menu items in our menu. This method is referred to as "translate" because a menu item translation set is created.

1. Add or edit a menu item for the first page (for example, **News** and articles), choose a language (for example, English), and save the menu item.

2. For the translated page (for example, **Nachrichten** and german-articles), follow the previous directions for nodes translated using the node translation model.

 If you create a new menu item directly, also choose the language for the page.

With the **Main menu** translated, the German version now looks similar to the following screenshot:

Taxonomy terms

In the previous chapter, we translated taxonomy term fields using the Entity Translation module. For a completely different approach, we can leverage the Taxonomy Translation module from the Internationalization package.

Before continuing, if the Multilingual Content module is installed, verify whether the **Switch interface for translating** checkbox is enabled at **Configuration | Regional and language | Multilingual settings | Node options** or you will see unexpected behavior in this section. For example, if you edit a German translation using the English UI, then you will only see English terms even though you would most likely want to see German terms.

Taxonomy translation module

The Taxonomy Translation module provides four different multilingual options depending on how we use our vocabularies and terms. The simplest choice is to use the default option and do nothing to a vocabulary or its terms. This makes sense if you have terms that are language-independent such as a list of programming languages (for example, HTML, Java, PHP, and so on) or companies (for example, Apple, HP, IBM, Microsoft, and so on).

Another option is to assign a fixed language to a vocabulary. This is useful if you have terms that only make sense in one language. For example, we might maintain a list of slang words per language as translating the slang might not be accurate. Other lists that might be separated by language are songs, videos, or other language-dependent media.

If you plan on having a term list where you add terms in the String Translation source language and then translate each term name and description, you can use the "localize" option. For example, you might maintain a list of colors, animals, plants, or ice cream flavors where each term will be translated for each language.

For the last option ("translate"), we can create a mixed-language vocabulary. For the slang example, we could create one "slang" vocabulary and put all slang terms for all languages in it. Then we can translate some slang terms (or not!). As long as we assign a language per term, the correct terms will be available for us when using the vocabulary. For example, when editing a node with slang terms, the Polish UI will only have access to the Polish slang terms.

To better visualize the four options available from the Taxonomy Translation module, take a look at the following figure. For the **Default** example, the term is language-independent. For the **Fixed** example, terms come from separate language-specific vocabularies. For the **Localize** example, there is one term "object", whereas for the **Translate** example, each translation is a separate term "object" with the translations forming a translation set. In the figure, **NT** stands for "node-translated" and **FT** stands for "field-translated".

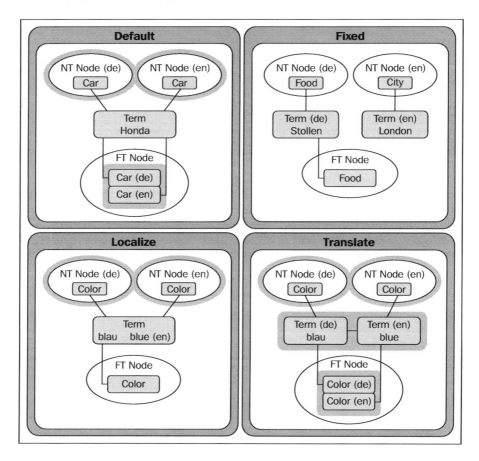

Language-independent terms

Let's start with the default option for a language-independent vocabulary:

1. Install the Taxonomy Translation module from the Internationalization package (`drupal.org/project/i18n`).

2. Now create a new vocabulary or choose an existing one. If you are using the demo site, there are several vocabularies such as **Blog Tags**, **Book Style**, **Drupal Level**, and **Drupal Version**. The **Drupal Version** vocabulary is a good choice here as the terms **Drupal 6**, **Drupal 7**, and so on will not be translated.

3. Also, make sure you have a content type with a taxonomy term reference field for that vocabulary. The demo site uses **Blog Tags** for **Blog entry** nodes and **Book Style**, **Drupal Level**, and **Drupal Version** for **Drupal Book** nodes.

4. Navigate to **Structure | Taxonomy** and click on the **edit vocabulary** link for your vocabulary. You'll see a **Multilingual options** section similar to the following screenshot:

The first option, **No multilingual options for terms**, is our default, and we'll use this for vocabularies with language-independent terms. We'll learn how to translate the vocabulary field label/name later in the chapter in case this is needed.

Language-specific terms

We can make a vocabulary language-specific, so that the vocabulary is only used for content in that language. In my case, I'll assume that the **Book Style** terms only make sense for English users.

1. Go to **Structure | Taxonomy** and click on the appropriate **edit vocabulary** link.

2. Choose **Fixed Language** and a **Language** drop-down field will be displayed.

3. Select the language and click on **Save**:

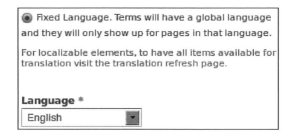

4. If you edit or view a node associated with that vocabulary, the terms will only show up if the term language matches the UI language. For example, when I view a German **Drupal Book** node, the **Book Style** terms are gone.

Localized terms

For vocabularies where terms will be added in the String Translation source language, we can use the **Localize** option. This option is called "localize" because it does not create term translation sets.

1. Choose a vocabulary to edit, select **Localize**, and click on **Save**. In my case, I'll edit **Drupal Level** at **Structure | Taxonomy | Drupal Level | Edit**.

 Make sure to start with terms in the String Translation source language, and then don't change the source language or translations might break!

2. Now edit a term (or add a new one and save) and there will be a **Translate** tab. Click on the tab to get the translation overview page for the term.

LANGUAGE	TITLE	STATUS	OPERATIONS
English (source)	Intermediate	original	edit
Arabic	Intermediate	not translated	translate
German	Intermediate	not translated	translate
Polish	Intermediate	not translated	translate

You can probably do this blindfolded now!

3. Click on **translate**, translate the **Name** and **Description** (if available), click on **Save translation**, and repeat for all languages.

4. Then repeat the process for all terms. It's tedious, but it works!

   Well, it will work. But, there are still a few more steps if we want the translated text to actually show up for our nodes.

5. Go to the **Manage display** page for a content type with the vocabulary. In my case, I'll go to the **Structure | Content types | Drupal Book | Manage display**.

6. By default, the format for the taxonomy term reference is set to **Link**. Change this to **Link (localized)** and click on **Save**.

7. Now if you edit or view a translated node with that vocabulary, the vocabulary terms will be appropriate for the language. I translated "Intermediate" to "Zwischen" for German. So if I view an **Intermediate** book while in German, the terms will appear as in the following screenshot:

 To translate your taxonomy terms faster, check out the Translation Table module. It provides a config page at **Configuration | Regional and language | Translate interface | Translation table** where you can translate many terms at once. It also helps with field labels, content type strings, and menu items.

Mixed-language vocabulary

For vocabularies with terms in multiple languages (with none, some, or all translated), the **Translate** option can be used. Unlike **Localize**, this option uses term translation sets and you don't have to add new terms in the String Translation source language.

1. Edit a vocabulary, select the **Translate** radio button, and click on **Save**. For example, the **Blog Tags** vocabulary would be a good choice since it is a free-form list of terms and not all terms may translate well to all languages.

2. Edit a term from your vocabulary and you will find a new **Language** field. Choose a language and then click on **Save and translate**. The translation overview page will show up for the term.

 The **Translate** tab page behaves differently depending on the multilingual option. With the **Localize** option, the page lets you update the name and description of a term for each language (you translate the user-defined strings). With the **Translate** option, the page lets you add a new term or select an existing term for each language (to associate with the source term and add to the translation set).

3. Now you have two options, that is you can either click on the **add translation** link or you can choose an existing term in the **Select translations** form.

4. Go through and create translations for some of your terms, and add new terms for specific languages only. The term list page will show the language associated with each term.

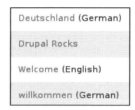

5. Now if you are editing a node associated with this vocabulary, only the relevant terms will appear. For example, if I am using the German interface and add a **Blog entry** node, I can choose **willkommen** but not **Welcome**. If I'm using the English interface, then **Deutschland** won't be available. Language-neutral terms are accessible for all languages.

Updating the field label

You might have noticed that the field label for our taxonomy term reference field (for example, **Blog Tags** or **Drupal Level**) is still in English. We'll need to translate it so that our field label language matches our interface language.

1. Install the Field Translation module from the Internationalization package (`drupal.org/project/i18n`). This module lets you translate field settings.

2. Go to the **Manage fields** page for the content type that has the taxonomy term reference field (for example, **Structure | Content types | Drupal Book | Manage fields**) and then click on **edit** for the term reference field (for example, **Drupal Level**).

3. You'll find the usual **Translate** tab. So click on it to see your overview table.

4. You should already know what to do. Click on the **translate** link for a language, translate the **Name** and **Description** text, click on **Save translation**, and then repeat for all languages and content types as needed.

5. Now when you are viewing nodes for these content types, the vocabulary label will also reflect the language.

Views

Although the Views module is not in Drupal core (yet!), pretty much every Drupal site uses Views to create custom content pages, blocks, feeds, and so on. We can use Views' built-in language support along with help from the Internationalization Views module to update or add views for a multilingual website. For each view, we'll need to decide if we want one view that handles multiple languages or multiple views, each handling one language. I'll assume you know how to use Views for this section.

Multilingual views

Let's start out with making a view that handles multiple languages:

1. First create or edit a view. For now, only work with nodes that use the node translation model. We'll look at field-translated nodes a bit later. For example, the demo site has an **articles** view that shows up on the **News** page (for example, **Structure | Views | Articles**).

2. Click on the **add** link in the **Filter criteria** section, and then search for "language" and you'll see a filter for **Content translation: Language.** Note that this filter only shows up if you have the core Content Translation module enabled.

3. Select the checkbox and click on **Add and configure filter criteria**.

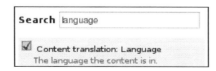

4. Now select the **Current user's language** checkbox and click on **Apply (all displays)**.

 If you want language-neutral nodes to show up as well, also select the **No language** checkbox.

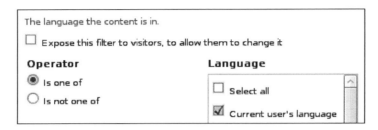

The language the content is in.

☐ Expose this filter to visitors, to allow them to change it

Operator

◉ Is one of

◯ Is not one of

Language

☐ Select all

☑ Current user's language

5. Save your view and go to the generated page (for example, /articles).

6. Switching languages with the language switcher will now cause the view to grab the nodes based on language. You'll see English nodes in the English UI, German nodes in the German UI, and so on. Simple!

 Strictly speaking, the "Current user's language" isn't necessarily the same as the interface language. If you don't have the Entity Translation module turned on, then it is the same. But, with Entity Translation enabled, the "Current user's language" is based on the content language settings at **Configuration | Regional and language | Languages | Detection and selection**. Since we configured content language detection to be the same as the interface language detection in the previous chapter, the end result is the same in our case.

For views pages, if you want different paths per language, you can install the i18n Page Views module (drupal.org/project/i18_page_views). You will need to choose the **i18n page** display rather than the **page** display to configure path settings for each language.

PAGE SETTINGS

Path in *Arabic*: news-arabic

Path in *English*: news

Path in *German*: news-german

Path in *Polish*: news-polish

Language-specific views

Creating a view for a specific language is similar to what we just did. This time, though, instead of choosing **Current user's language** for the **Content translation: Language** filter, just choose the desired language. This method is useful if you want to show a different view for each language or a special view for a subset of languages. This method works for nodes translated using the node translation method.

1. Edit the previous view and change the language filter to use one language and save the view.

2. Now when you look at the output, it will only show nodes for the chosen language. For example, if you configured the view for English, then you will see English nodes no matter what the interface language is.

3. To create multiple views for different languages, just add a new page display and change the language, URL path, and other fields as desired.

4. Now you can add these URLs to your navigation. For example, you can add them to a multilingual menu like we did earlier in the chapter.

Nodes using field translation

The previous examples used translated nodes where there is a different node per language. Things work a bit differently when dealing with nodes using the field translation model since there is only one node. The single node has a language associated with it which is the source language. Individual fields are then translated from the source language into other languages.

When using the Views' language filter for field-translated nodes, the source language is analyzed. So, if we configure a view to use the **Current user's language** option and switch to English, only nodes with the source language of English show up. If we switch to German, only nodes with the German source language show up, even if there is a German translation of an English node. The workaround is to not use the **Content translation: Language** filter and, instead, use an option provided by the Entity Translation module.

1. Add or edit a view and, if necessary, remove the **Content translation: Language** filter.

2. Click on **Advanced** and look for the **Field Language** option in the **Other** section.

3. Configure the **Field Language**, choose **Current user's language**, and select the **When needed, add the field language condition to the query** checkbox.

4. Click on **Apply** and save the view.

 If you are using the node title as a view field, you need to use the title provided by the Title module rather than the core title marked with "The content title".

Now the view will behave as expected. For example, you will see the German translation of a node (if it's available) from the German interface. If you have the fallback option enabled at **Configuration | Regional and language | Entity translation**, then the source content will be shown when there is no translation available.

 At the time of writing, if you want to show some node-translated nodes and some field-translated nodes in the same view, then this isn't possible out-of-the-box. Instead you could write custom code to handle it.

Non-node views

Views can be configured for non-node content including comments, taxonomy terms, and users. This section quickly runs through example configurations for these types of views.

Comments

When creating a view, we can choose to show comments rather than nodes. For example, we can create a views block containing the most recent comments that are associated with nodes in a particular language. Let's try that out:

1. Create a new view, choose **Comments** for the **Show** list, deselect the **Create a page** checkbox, and select the **Create a block** checkbox.

2. Now choose **HTML list** and **fields** in the **Display format** section and click on **Continue & edit**.

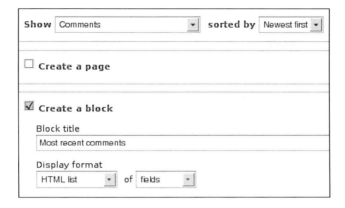

The rest of the configuration is the same as with the node view.

3. Add the **Content translation: Language** filter and choose **Current user's language**.

4. Save the view and put the block on your site.

The block will only show comments that are associated with nodes that have been created in the chosen language. For example, when viewing German content, the comments will be displayed for German nodes regardless of the comment language. At the time of writing, views cannot be configured to show comments based on the comment language.

Taxonomy terms

For taxonomy terms configured with the Taxonomy Translation module (discussed earlier in this chapter), we can create a view for terms that is similar to the recent comments block by choosing **Taxonomy terms** rather than **Comments** in the **Show** list. But, there is no default language filter available for taxonomy terms. Not to worry!

1. Install the Internationalization Views module (`drupal.org/project/i18nviews`). The project is called Internationalization Views but the actual module is called Views Translation.

2. Now you'll have a new **Taxonomy term: Language** filter available. Add the filter and configure it by choosing **Current user's language**.

3. Then save the view and you'll have a block that shows the most recent terms for the interface language.

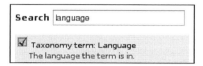

For taxonomy terms that are configured for field translation (discussed in the previous chapter), we cannot use the **Taxonomy term: Language** filter and, instead, need to use the **Advanced / Field Language** option like we used for field-translated nodes.

 If you add the term name field to the view, use the name field that is provided by the Title module rather than the core name field marked with the description **The taxonomy term name**. Similarly, for the term description, use the field called **Taxonomy term: Description** provided by the Title module rather than the core **Taxonomy term: Term description** field. This is definitely confusing! One of the goals of Drupal 8 is to eliminate the need for the Title module, which would make things simpler.

Users

A realistic views use case for users would be to show the most recent users based on their profile language. Creating this block has steps similar to those for the recent comments or terms blocks.

1. When adding the view, choose **Users** in the **Show** list and then add the **User: Language** filter and choose the **Current user's language** option.

2. Save the view, place the block as desired, and then the users in the block will match the interface language.

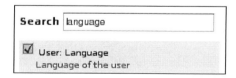

In the previous chapter, we added a user "Bio" field and configured it for field translation. To show users with this "Bio" field, we wouldn't use the **User: Language** filter but, instead, would use the **Advanced / Field Language** option like we did earlier for field-translated nodes. Then, we would see user "Bio" translations when switching between languages.

Views text

In addition to handling content generated from a views query, we can translate strings associated with a view including title, header, footer, and empty text with the help of the Internationalization Views/Views Translation module.

1. Go to **Structure | Views** and you'll find a **translate** link in the **Operations** list for each view:

2. Click on **translate** to get to the translation overview page. Then you can translate views strings for each display and language with the usual process.

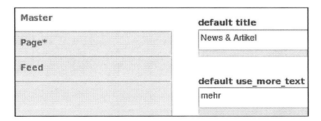

Look at your views page in another language and you'll see translated views text. Easy!

Summary

Now you know how to configure the standard components of a multilingual Drupal site! Here's a brief review of what we learned in this chapter.

We started off with configuring blocks by creating a block associated with one language. Then, title and body text were translated for a custom block and for the **Powered by Drupal** block provided by a module.

Then, we moved onto menus. A language-specific menu was created, and we localized and translated different types of menu items to make a multilingual menu.

After blocks and menus, we used the Taxonomy Translation module to create language-specific and multilingual vocabularies and terms.

The last part of the chapter focused on Views configuration by creating multilingual and language-specific views. Different language settings were used for node-translated and field-translated content, and language-aware views were created for comments, taxonomy terms, and users. The chapter concluded with translating views strings (for example, title and header text) with the help of the Internationalization Views module.

Guess what? Only one chapter to go. Let's learn some advanced topics!

5
Panels, SEO, and More!

In the previous chapter, we configured the common Drupal components: blocks, menus, taxonomy, and views. In this chapter, we'll explore several final topics for our multilingual Drupal 7 website.

First, we'll discuss creating multilingual and language-specific panels. After panels, we will look at some Search Engine Optimization (SEO) tips and the language support for the top Drupal 7 SEO modules. The chapter concludes by examining a few subjects that might also apply to your Drupal site such as content translation management and workflow, theming, and custom module development.

Panels

Although it's not as popular as Views, the Panels module has a reported usage of more than 100,000 installs! Not too shabby. If you haven't tried Panels yet, it's a little hard to wrap your head around it at first when you are used to Drupal's built-in block configuration. But, if you are willing to take the plunge, you'll find that Panels is an awesome tool for sites with non-standard or multiple layout requirements. David Mercer's Drupal 7 book has an introduction to Panels, but, for more in-depth coverage, Bhavin (Vin) Patel has a Drupal Panels book and Earl and Lynette Miles wrote one for Panels, CCK, and Views. I'll assume you know how to use Panels for this section.

Panel panes

The language behavior of panel panes depends on the pane content. For example, if you add a multilingual block, then you will see the language-specific block content when viewing the panel with another language. This is the same for any component added to a pane including nodes, menus, variables, and forms. In my case, I created a panel page that included the **Powered by Drupal** block, **Who's online** block, site name, "Multilingual Drupal rocks" blog post, the contact form, and a custom footer menu. When viewing the panel page in German, all of these components are translated accordingly. Awesome!

At the time of writing, one issue with multilingual panel panes is how to deal with titles. You can override a pane title if you want to, but then how do you translate that title? Well, fortunately, people have been working on that problem and there is a patch that works. Follow the issue at `drupal.org/node/1179034`.

1. I applied the patch, saved the panel page again, and flushed the caches. Now there is a new **Panels** text group available on the **Configuration | Regional and language | Translate interface | Translate** page.

2. Just choose this text group and click **Filter** and you'll see all the Panels-related strings you can translate.

TEXT GROUP	STRING	CONTEXT	LANGUAGES	OPER
Panels	This is powered by Drupal block panels:pane_configuration:1:title	pane_configuration:1:title	~~ar de pl~~	edit
Panels	Multilingual panel page panels:display_configuration:1:title	display_configuration:1:title	~~ar de pl~~	edit

Language-specific panel pages

If you want different panel pages per language, there is currently no way to set the language of the panel page. But, you can create a translation set for your panel pages by using the Path Translation module as follows:

1. Create separate panel pages per language with unique paths.
2. Install the Path Translation module from the Internationalization package (`drupal.org/project/i18n`).
3. Go to **Configuration** | **Regional and language** | **Translation sets** | **Paths**.
4. Click on the **Add path translation** link.
5. Fill in paths for each language and click the **Save** button.

Now the language switcher will know what links to use for each language.

TITLE	ITEMS	CREATED
Panel pages translation set	i18n-panel-page-german i18n-panel-page-english	01/22/2012 - 13:29

> The Path Translation module is not specific to Panels. You can use it for Views pages or custom pages created with a module. It is not needed for node content.

SEO

Search Engine Optimization (SEO) is vital for every website that wants free traffic from search engines (which is pretty much all sites!). If you haven't yet, you should check out *Drupal Search Engine Optimization, Ben Finklea, Packt Publishing*, as it covers the basics. In this section, we'll look at some multilingual and international SEO tips and how to configure the most common SEO modules for a multilingual Drupal 7 site. If you are looking for more modules, check out `kristen.org/drupal-seo-modules`.

Multilingual and international SEO

Multilingual SEO addresses multilingual sites. International SEO assumes that our site will have users in more than one country. These are parallel concerns as our site can cater to multiple languages and one country or to multiple countries and one language.

The following are a few things to consider when dealing with multilingual and international SEO:

- The same SEO principles generally apply regardless of language/country
- Evaluate all SEO requirements at the start of a project
- Avoid automated translation due to poor quality
- When possible, use native translators for your target countries
- Don't translate keywords. Do keyword research per language/country
- Avoid using the same content across languages (or set up proper redirects)
- Each page should focus on one language (that is, avoid mixing languages)
- Avoid culture-specific content or technical jargon that doesn't translate well
- Enable URL detection so there are language-specific URLs or domains
- In some cases, use country-specific domains when possible
- Check your web analytics to see what countries you should be targeting
- Create separate webmaster tools accounts for all site languages/countries
- Learn what the top search engines for your target countries are
- Use keyword research tools with data for the target languages/countries
- Set the geographical meta data for region-specific pages
- Get links from other sites within the same region/country

Now let's move on to configuring the most important Drupal 7 SEO modules.

Friendly URLs

If you're not using Pathauto, you should be. Pathauto lets you set user- and SEO-friendly patterns for your URLs. For example, instead of a cryptic `/node/55` URL, you can use Pathauto to use the content title so it becomes `/articles/multilingual-drupal-7`, which is human-readable and contains relevant keywords.

Pathauto works fine for nodes using the node translation model as each language has a separate node. At the time of writing, for field translation, the Pathauto and Entity Translation module maintainers have been ironing out some issues. To get the automatic URL aliases to work in Drupal 7 for field-translated nodes, you must use at least Entity Translation version 7.x-1.0-alpha2, if available, or the most recent dev version.

If you want language-specific URL patterns, Pathauto lets you set those for node pages.

1. Install the Pathauto module (`drupal.org/project/pathauto`).

2. Go to **Configuration** | **Search and metadata** | **URL aliases** | **Patterns**, fill in the patterns for each language in the **Content paths** section, and click **Save configuration**. Blank patterns will use the default pattern.

3. To override the pattern for a node, edit the node, unselect **Generate automatic URL alias**, fill in the **URL alias** field, and save. Simple!

> When specifying aliases and alias patterns, do not include the language's path prefix or domain. For example, a URL alias might be about (not de/about) and an alias pattern might be article/[node:title] (not de/article/[node:title]).

If you already have nodes using field translation, you'll need to edit each translation, select the **Generate automatic URL alias** checkbox, and click **Save translation**. This is unfortunate, but required. Perhaps someone will write the code to help with that! Maybe you?

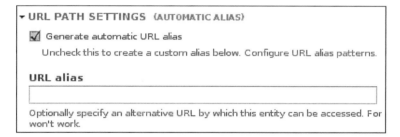

Removing special characters from path aliases

For some languages, there are interesting characters such as ä, ß, and é mixed in with Roman characters, and, for other languages, the characters look nothing like any in the Roman alphabet. After installing Pathauto, the default rules are set up so the path alias is created from the node title, for example content/[node:title]. So, if your node title has non-Roman characters in it, then you will get an alias that includes those characters.

For example, if my Pathauto blog content type pattern is `blog/[node:author]/[node:title]` and I create a blog post called "*Typing Umlauts ä ö ü ß Ä Ö Ü*", then the path alias looks like the following:

URL alias

blog/kristen/typing-umlauts-ä-ö-ü-ß-ä-ö-ü

These special characters are not user-friendly and aren't optimal for search engines either. To get rid of them:

1. Install the Transliteration module (`drupal.org/project/transliteration`) and go to **Configuration | Search and metadata | URL aliases | Settings**.

2. Select the **Transliterate prior to creating alias** checkbox.

3. Click on **Save configuration**.

> ☑ Transliterate prior to creating alias
>
> When a pattern includes certain characters (such as those with accents) should Pathauto attempt to transliterate them into the ASCII-96 alphabet? Transliteration is handled by the Transliteration module.

Now if you go back to a node with special characters in its alias, you can edit and save it with the **Generate automatic URL alias** option enabled. The path will be updated so the non-Roman characters are replaced with Roman characters. In my case, my new node alias is now: `blog/kristen/typing-umlauts-o-u-ss-o-u`. Note that the a was removed from the alias because of the default **Strings to Remove** settings at **Configuration | Search and metadata | URL aliases | Settings**.

Page title and meta tags

The `<title>` tag text (AKA "page title") shows up at the top of the browser and is often used in search engine results. It's super important SEO text! In Drupal 7, you can use the Meta Tags module or the Page Title module to add `<title>` tags.

Cool Multilingual Drupal 7 Book!

A meta tag is HTML text that shows up in the `<head>` section of your web page using the `<meta>` notation. These tags are mainly used to relay information to search engine crawlers such as the page's description, keywords, robot settings, and so on. Although adding meta keywords for your web pages is no longer necessary, meta tags are still useful for SEO.

In particular, the description meta tag should be added to your content so that your search results can have the best possible summary text. The meta description is essentially your marketing message telling everyone: *"This is the content you want!"*

In Drupal 7, you can choose from the Meta Tags and the Meta Tags Quick modules for your meta tags. At the time of writing, the main differences between the two modules are as follows:

- Meta Tags Quick is field-based and Meta Tags has a custom architecture
- Meta Tags handles page titles and default global meta tags

Meta Tags module

In previous Drupal versions, we used the Nodewords module for meta tags but, for Drupal 7, Nodewords has been rewritten and has a more intuitive name: Meta Tags. Like with Pathauto, the Meta Tags module works as expected with node-translated content. Unfortunately, at the time of writing, Entity Translation support is not available for Meta Tags. Smart people have been working on it, though, so track the issue at `drupal.org/node/1282620`. And, you can help out too by fixing and testing patches.

1. Install the Meta Tags module (`drupal.org/project/metatag`) and enable Meta Tag API and Meta Tag UI.

2. To add meta tag patterns, navigate to the **Configuration | Search and metadata | Meta tags** config page and add or override patterns as needed.

3. To use custom meta tag text for a node (recommended for at least your top pages), just edit the node content as usual, click the **Meta tags** tab towards the bottom of the form, and fill in the description, keywords (optional), and page title.

Description

Multilingual Drupal 7 is an awesome book about Drupal internationalization and localization!

A brief and concise summary of the page's content, preferrably 150 characters or less. The

Meta Tags Quick module

Meta Tags Quick is new for Drupal 7 and uses fields for the meta tags. The nice thing about this is that field-based meta tags work for both node-translated and field-translated nodes. Yeah!

1. Install the Meta Tags Quick module (`drupal.org/project/metatags_quick`) and enable Meta Tags (Quick). To avoid confusion, disable the Meta Tags modules.

2. The module is easy to use. Just enable it and then navigate to **Configuration | Search and metadata | Meta tags (quick) settings**.

3. Check the boxes for the meta tag fields you want added to each entity and click the **Attach** button. For example, if you choose **Description** and **Keywords** for the **Node** entity, then all the content types will have a meta description and a meta keywords field added.

BUNDLE/ENTITY	ABSTRACT	COPYRIGHT	DESCRIPTION	KEYWORDS
Node	☐	☐	✓	✓
Taxonomy term	☐	☐	✓	✓
Comment	☐	☐	☐	☐

4. Then when you look at the content type's fields or edit a node, the meta tag fields are listed.

(Meta)Description

Multilingual Drupal 7 is an awesome book on Drupal 7 internationalization and localization

Page Title module

In previous versions of Drupal, we used the Page Title module to set the `<title>` tag for content. If you are using the Meta Tags module, you can set a default page title pattern for all pages and override page titles for entities. If you are using Meta Tags Quick, then you definitely need the Page Title module for page titles.

For nodes using node translation, Page Title works fine since each language has its own node. At the time of writing, though, field-translated nodes aren't currently supported. You can track this issue here: `drupal.org/node/1264024`.

1. Install the Page Title module (`drupal.org/project/page_title`).

2. To manage Page Title patterns, go to **Configuration | Search and metadata | Page titles**. There are plans to allow language-specific patterns like what Pathauto provides (`drupal.org/node/383358`).

3. To override a page title, just fill in the Page Title text in the node edit form and save. Easy!

Page title
Cool Multilingual Drupal 7 Book!

Home page optimization

In *Chapter 3*, *Working with Content*, we used the Multilingual Select module to make sure the default /node home page showed content based on our selected language. Most sites won't use the /node page and will, instead, replace it with a page from Views, Panels, or custom code. In this case, for optimal SEO, make sure to either have one home page that handles each language correctly or create a separate home page for each language.

For the latter, since the home page path is handled with a site variable, you'll need to use the variable translation process like how we did for **Site name** in *Chapter 2*, *Setting up the Basics: Languages, UI Translation, and System Settings*.

1. Make sure the Variable Translation and Variable modules are enabled.

2. Go to **Configuration | Regional and language | Multilingual settings | Variables**, check the **Default front page** checkbox, and save the settings.

3. Then, go to **Configuration | System | Site information**, click on a language in the **Select language** list, update the **Default front page** field with the home page for that language, and click on **Save configuration**.

4. Repeat for all languages.

Duplicate pages

Search engines don't like seeing the exact same content on different pages. The default Drupal setup lets you access the same page with more than one path. For example, if /node/5 is aliased to /about-us, then these paths will show duplicate content:

- /node/5
- /node/5/
- /about-us
- /about-us/

For Drupal 7, the typical remedy is to install the Global Redirect and Redirect modules. The Redirect module has incorporated the Path Redirect module functionality from Drupal 6 and will eventually replace Global Redirect as well.

 At the time of writing, there are serious redirect issues in Global Redirect version 7.x-1.4 and below when used on multilingual sites. Do not use Global Redirect until these issues have been resolved. And, when you do use it, back up your database and try it on a development server first. For more info, search for "language" at `drupal.org/project/issues/globalredirect`.

If you install Global Redirect (read the previous warning), go to **Configuration | System | Global Redirect**, select the **Language Path Checking** checkbox, and click on **Save Configuration**.

With translation added to the mix, we have more duplicate pages even when content has been translated. For example, if German and Polish are enabled and we are using node translation, then there will be duplicate content at `/node/5`, `/de/node/5`, and `/pl/node/5`.

Translated nodes can be handled by enabling the Multilingual Content and Translation Redirect modules from the Internationalization package. Translation Redirect actually won't do any redirection by itself. It needs Multilingual Content to determine what the translation page is for a particular node. So, for the previous example, if we translate `/node/5` into German using node translation and get a new `/node/12` page, then the redirection will work as follows (assuming, for the moment, Global Redirect is not on):

- User requests `/node/5` and no redirection happens (English is shown)
- User requests `/de/node/5` and is redirected to `/de/node/12` (German is shown)
- User requests `/pl/node/5` and no redirection happens (English is shown)

Note that currently the redirection will only happen for anonymous users though this may be made configurable in the future. Also, the home page is not redirected by design since sites should explicitly use a language-aware home page.

At the time of writing, there is no redirection support for field-translated nodes. This is fine if there are translations for all languages or if the Entity Translation module's language fallback is disabled. If the fallback option is enabled and you are missing translations, then the search engines will see the same content at different URLs.

The search engines are usually smart enough to figure out which is the source content because it can check if the meta tag language matches the language of the actual content. So, this isn't usually a big problem, but something you should keep in mind.

Translation management and workflow

Content management and workflow can be simple or complex depending on the website. One site might have content authors who are allowed to publish content themselves, while another might require a moderation cycle involving different reviewers. With a translation step added, things get more interesting, particularly if there are many languages involved. This section covers some options for handling translation management and workflow in Drupal 7.

Who can translate?

You should decide at the beginning of your project who will be translating the content. Do you have one person to do all the work, or will you have a team of translators? Will it be done by employees, or outsourced to a translation company? Or maybe both?

Even if you initially intend to only have one translator, it is a good practice to create a translator role since you can then assign appropriate permissions to that role. It's possible you will need more fine-grained roles depending on your site, such as a blog translator role and a product translator role or a content translator role and an interface translator role. Make sure to set your module permissions appropriately for your roles. The *Appendix, Modules, Resources, and Getting Involved*, lists the permissions associated for all the modules used in the book.

Content administration

The core **Find content** admin page (`/admin/content`) lets you find node content based on language. Just choose a language and click on **Filter**. If more advanced filtering is needed, this page can be replaced with one built with Views and Views Bulk Operations.

If you want to set the language for one or more nodes using the content admin form, the Language Assignment module will help once it's ready for Drupal 7 (drupal.org/node/1086454). Another handy module is Administration Language that lets administrators see all admin pages in a preferred language.

To flag content for translation, there is an option available in the **Translation settings** on the node content edit form. If you are editing the source content, you can select the **Flag translations as outdated** checkbox and, if you are editing a translation, you can select the **This translation needs to be updated** checkbox. In both cases, if you select the checkbox and save the content, you will see an **outdated** flag on the translation overview page.

| German | Mehrsprachige Drupal-Felsen! | Published - outdated | edit |

Contributed modules

Two translation management modules that have been contributed to Drupal 7 are Lingotek Collaborative Translation and Translation Management Tool.

Lingotek Collaborative Translation module

Lingotek Collaborative Translation is maintained by Lingotek (lingotek.com) and has an interesting twist. You can use your own in-house translators, submit content to Lingotek for translation, use automatic translation tools, and leverage your users to voluntarily translate content for you. This last method is known as "*translation crowdsourcing*" and is all the rage. Social networking giants like Facebook and Twitter are getting content translated this way. So, if you think your users might contribute translations, try out the module and see what you think. There are demos and documentation available at lingotek.com/drupal.

Translation Management Tool module

The first Drupal translation management module, Translation Management, was created by ICanLocalize (icanlocalize.com) for Drupal 6. At the time of writing, the Drupal 7 port for the module had stalled. So, in early 2012, a bunch of committed Drupalers got together in Zurich for a code sprint. Initially, they planned to update the Translation Management module for Drupal 7 but they found it was best to start from scratch. The Translation Management Tool module is the result of their hard work. Help with making this new module great by testing and participating in the issue queue!

Custom workflow

If you decide, for whatever reason, that you want to build your own custom translation workflow, Drupal has all the tools you need for the job. You'll have some configuring to do, but, in the end, it will be just how you want it. There are plenty of modules that can help with this, including multilingual-specific ones like Translation Access and Translation Overview and general ones such as Rules, Workflow, Revisioning, Scheduler, and the new Workbench suite.

The general modules can be used for regular content management and workflow out-of-the-box but, at the time of writing, setting them up for multilingual content will require some custom coding. Once multilingual support has been finished for the Rules module (`drupal.org/node/1422996`), creating a custom translation workflow should be much easier.

Theming and module development

Every Drupal site uses a theme (or two!). It can be a free core or contributed theme. You can buy one from a theme vendor, for example, `topnotchthemes.com` or `themesnap.com`. Or, you can get fancy and create your own! In this section, we'll look at some considerations for multilingual theming including RTL support and custom CSS.

Many developers create modules to handle custom site features. This section also briefly covers internationalization for custom modules, including using string functions for hard-coded and user-defined strings. To learn more about theme and module development, check out the Drupal 7 Themes book by Ric Shreves and the Drupal 7 Module Development book by Matt Butcher, Larry Garfield, John Wilkins, Matt Farina, Ken Rickard, and Greg Dunlap.

RTL support

If you plan to use a Right-to-Left (RTL) language such as Arabic or Hebrew, your theme must have RTL support for the site to display properly in that language. All Drupal core themes have this support. To find other RTL-capable themes, you can perform a theme search at `drupal.org/project/themes` using the text "rtl" in the **Search Themes** text field.

These themes have CSS stylesheets to handle the Right-to-Left layout. For example, if you look at the core `Bartik` theme files, the stylesheets include `layout.css`, `layout-rtl.css`, `style.css`, `style-rtl.css`, `ie.css`, and `ie-rtl.css`.

If your site uses a custom theme, you'll need to add these RTL CSS files if they haven't been created. Creating Right-to-Left stylesheets involves changing floats, padding, and margins so that the layout is flipped. For example, the main menu might be floated left for the Left-to-Right (LTR) layout and floated right for RTL. You can check out what the experts have done by peeking at the core themes.

Interface and content languages

There is an "interface language" that is determined using the interface language detection settings at **Configuration | Regional and language | Languages | Detection and selection**. There is a "content language" as well since sometimes we want to show content in a different language than the UI (for example, when using a search form). When the Entity Translation module isn't used, the content language is the same as the interface language. But, when using Entity Translation, the content language is determined with the content language detection settings on the **Detection and selection** page.

If you want to know the interface and content languages, you can use the global `$language` and `$language_content` variables, which are objects that include the language's code, name, directionality, and so on. If you are just interested in the language's code, you can write some PHP like the following:

```
global $language, $language_content;
$interface_langcode = $language->language;
$content_langcode = $language_content->language;
```

To analyze these objects, use `var_dump()` or `devel_print_object()` if the Devel module is installed.

Custom CSS

We often want to add custom CSS whether or not we have a multilingual site. If you're using a custom theme, then it is simple to add or change the CSS. If you are using a core or contributed theme, then it is not as simple because you should **not** change the theme's CSS files or your changes will be wiped out when updating the theme. Not good!

If you already have a custom module or know how to create one, you can add your CSS using the `drupal_add_css` function. For example, if we want to create CSS to remove the bullets in the language switcher, we could create a custom module as follows:

1. Create a module directory, for example, `sites/all/modules/custom/my_demo`.

2. Create a `.info` file in the module directory, for example, `my_demo.info`:

```
name = My Demo
description = My demo module
core = 7.x
```

3. Create a `.module` file in the module directory, for example, `my_demo.module`:

```php
<?php
function my_demo_init() {
  $path = drupal_get_path('module', 'my_demo');
  $css = $path . '/my_demo.css';
  drupal_add_css($css);
}
```

4. Create a `.css` file in the module directory, for example, `my_demo.css`:

```
#block-locale-language ul,
#block-locale-language-content ul {padding-left:0;}
#block-locale-language li,
#block-locale-language-content li {list-style:none;}
```

5. Create a RTL `.css` file in the module directory, for example, `my_demo-rtl.css`:

```
#block-locale-language ul,
#block-locale-language-content ul {padding-right:0;}
```

6. Enable the module and flush all caches.

Pretty easy, huh? With this tiny module enabled, the bullets will be removed from language switcher block links whether you are using an LTR or RTL language.

 One way to add new CSS files without writing any PHP code is to use the CSS Injector module.

String translation functions

If you are working with a custom theme or module, you'll need to use the `format_plural()` and `t()` functions for hard-coded strings and the `i18n_string()` function for user-defined strings. Hard-coded strings are ones that are contained within code in themes or modules. For example, if you want a custom admin block, we can update our previous module example by adding the following code to the `my_demo.module` file:

```
function my_demo_block_info() { // implement hook_block_info
  $blocks['my-demo-admin-block'] = array(
    'info' => t('This demo block shows info for the admins.'),
  );
  return $blocks;
}

function my_demo_block_view($delta = '') { // implement hook_block_view
  $block = array();
  switch ($delta) {
    case 'my-demo-admin-block':
      $block['subject'] = NULL;
      $block['content'] = theme('my_demo_admin_block');
      return $block;
  }
}

function my_demo_theme() { // implement hook_theme
  return array(
    'my_demo_admin_block' => array(
      'variables' => array(),
    ),
  );
}

function theme_my_demo_admin_block() { // custom theme function
  return '<span>' . t('Admins rock!') . '</span>';
}
```

 Drupal assumes that the text in your themes and modules is in English, so translation is always *from* English *to* the target language. There is no way to change this behavior.

User-defined strings are added via the UI such as taxonomy terms, content type names, and block titles. If we have code that deals with user-defined strings, we can't use the `t()` function but the Internationalization module provides an `i18n_string()` function that we can use instead. For example, if we want to show all the content types in our block, we could change the code as follows:

```
function theme_my_demo_admin_block() {
  $content_types = node_type_get_types();
  foreach ($content_types as $type => $type_object) {
    $key = 'node:type:' . $type . ':name';
    $name = $type_object->name;
    if (function_exists('i18n_string')) {
      $name = i18n_string($key, $name);
    }
    $type_url_str = str_replace('_', '-', $type);
    $links[] = '<li>' . l($name, 'node/add/' . $type_url_str) . '</li>';
  }
  return '<ul>' . implode('', $links) . '</ul>';
}
```

The `$key`, for example, `node:type:blog:name`, is a unique identifier and can be found using the form at **Configuration | Regional and language | Translate interface | Translate**.

 If you're writing JavaScript, then translate functions are available for hard-coded strings: `Drupal.formatPlural()` and `Drupal.t()`. The Localization API docs go into depth on these functions (and more!) at `drupal.org/node/322729`.

Summary

We did it! Let's do a quick recap of this chapter.

First, we learned we don't need to do anything special for multilingual panels, but do need to use the Path Translation module for panel translation sets. Then, we took a look at some multilingual and international SEO tips and the top Drupal 7 SEO modules for friendly URLs, page titles, meta tags, and handling duplicate content.

After panels and SEO, we discussed translation management and workflow including specialized roles, administration functionality, and contributed modules. The chapter concluded with a brief look at theming and module development including Right-to-Left theme support, custom CSS, and string translation functions.

Well, we're done! I hope you enjoyed yourself. Have fun with your multilingual Drupal 7 website!

Modules, Resources, and Getting Involved

Here are some of the great resources available for creating your multilingual Drupal 7 website. The modules used for the book exercises are listed with their permissions and project pages. There is also a list of additional modules that you might want to try out as well as community documentation and support groups to get your questions answered. We'll also take a look at how you can get involved in the Drupal community and what's in the works for Drupal 8 improvements. Don't forget to check the Drupal glossary at `drupal.org/glossary` if there are any Drupal words that you aren't familiar with.

Modules used in the book

Even with only about 50 multilingual Drupal 7 modules, it would take more space than we have in this book to explain each one. This section lists the modules covered in the book exercises, while additional multilingual modules are split out in another section.

The modules given are grouped alphabetically within the chapters where they are discussed. The following descriptions are intentionally brief. If you want more information about a module, its `drupal.org` project page has been provided for reference.

The module versions used are listed on the demo installation profile page (`drupal.org/project/multilingual_book_demo`). Also, module names have been standardized to use proper name casing as per the new Drupal policy (`drupal.org/node/1346158`).

Chapter 2

- **Contact Translation**: Allows you to create multilingual site contact forms via the Contact module. Project page: `drupal.org/project/i18n`. Permissions: `administer contact forms, access site-wide contact form`.

- **Internationalization**: Extends Drupal core multilingual functionality with a collection of submodules, mainly for configuration and translation support. These submodules are listed separately throughout this module list (marked with the same Drupal project URL). Project page: `drupal.org/project/i18n`.

- **Locale**: Adds basic language support and allows Drupal UI translation for languages besides English. Project page: `drupal.org/project/drupal` (core). Permissions: `administer languages, translate interface`.

- **Localization Client**: Provides a UI tool to fix interface translations and contribute them back to the community. Project page: `drupal.org/project/l10n_client`. Permissions: `use on-page translation, submit translations to localization server`.

- **Localization Update**: Grabs the latest translations for your site from `localize.drupal.org` or other localization servers. Project page: `drupal.org/project/l10n_update`. Permissions: `translate interface`.

- **String Overrides**: Provides a simple administration form so that any translatable text on the site can be changed for any language. Project page: `drupal.org/project/stringoverrides`. Permissions: `administer string overrides`.

- **Variable Translation**: Enables the translation of variables that are exposed via the Variable module such as the site's name and slogan. Project page: `drupal.org/project/i18n`. Permissions: `administer site configuration`.

Chapter 3

- **Content Translation**: Adds the ability to flag content types as translatable, so that content of those types can be handled using the node translation model. Project page: `drupal.org/project/drupal` (core). Permissions: `Translate content`.

- **Entity Translation**: Provides a UI for translating entity fields into multiple languages using the field translation model. Project page: `drupal.org/project/entity_translation`. Permissions: `translate any entity, administer entity translation, toggle field translatability`.

- **Multilingual Content**: Extends the content type and system multilingual settings with some helpful options such as making language selection required for nodes. Project page: `drupal.org/project/i18n`. Permissions: `administer site configuration`, `administer content translations`.

- **Multilingual Select**: Allows for core node listing pages to be filtered by language such as the default home page and the taxonomy pages. Project page: `drupal.org/project/i18n`. Permissions: `administer site configuration`.

- **Synchronize Translations**: Keeps data synchronized across translated nodes for fields that should be the same for all languages. Project page: `drupal.org/project/i18n`. Permissions: `administer site configuration`.

- **Title**: Creates a "real" title field for entities so that, when using field translation, titles can be translated like other fields. Project page: `drupal.org/project/title`. Permissions: `administer site configuration`.

Chapter 4

- **Block Languages**: Adds language options to the block visibility settings and provides support for translating block title and body content. Project page: `drupal.org/project/i18n`. Permissions: `translate interface`.

- **Field Translation**: Despite the name, this module supports translating field settings such as labels and help text rather than field values. Project page: `drupal.org/project/i18n`. Permissions: `administer site configuration`.

- **i18n Page Views**: Extra options for Views displays, so that paths can be specified for multiple languages. Project page: `drupal.org/project/i18_page_views`. Permissions: `Administer views`.

- **Internationalization Views**: Adds Views multilingual support such as allowing header, footer, and empty text to be translated. The project is Internationalization Views but the module it provides is called Views Translation. Project page: `drupal.org/project/i18nviews`. Permissions: `translate interface`, `administer views`.

- **Menu Translation**: Allows for language-specific and translated menus. Project page: `drupal.org/project/i18n`. Permissions: `administer menu`.

- **String Translation**: Leveraged by other modules for translating user-defined strings. Project page: `drupal.org/project/i18n`. Permissions: `translate interface`, `administer site configuration`, `use on-page translation`.

- **Taxonomy Translation**: Provides a number of options when configuring taxonomy vocabularies such as language-specific vocabularies and translatable terms. Project page: `drupal.org/project/i18n`. Permissions: `administer taxonomy`, `translate interface`.

Chapter 5

- **Path Translation**: Provides a mechanism to specify paths that are in a translation set which can be used for non-node pages such as the ones from Views or Panels. Project page: `drupal.org/project/i18n`. Permissions: `administer site configuration`.

- **Panels**: This isn't a multilingual module, but multilingual panel pages are discussed in this chapter. Project page: `drupal.org/project/panels`. Permissions: `use panels dashboard`, `administer page manager`, `administer site configuration`.

- **SEO-related modules**: These are not multilingual modules, but several Drupal 7 SEO modules are covered in this chapter, including the following:
    - **Global Redirect**: `drupal.org/project/globalredirect`
    - **Meta Tags**: `drupal.org/project/metatag`
    - **Meta Tags Quick**: `drupal.org/project/metatags_quick`
    - **Page Title**: `drupal.org/project/page_title`
    - **Pathauto**: `drupal.org/project/pathauto`
    - **Redirect**: `drupal.org/project/redirect`

- **Translation Redirect**: Helps with SEO by ensuring search engines are redirected to the appropriate translated pages. Project page: `drupal.org/project/i18n`.

- **Transliteration**: Replaces special characters in strings with Roman characters for cleaner URLs and filenames. Project page: `drupal.org/project/transliteration`. Permissions: `administer site configuration`.

Module usage

For some topics, separate modules are used to handle the translation process differently. Also, some modules have multiple configuration options. The following table serves as an overview of the key multilingual modules used in the book:

Topic	Module	Usage notes	Pages
Node	Locale	Assign language to node	42
Node	Content Translation	Translate nodes; node translation set	44-45
Node	Synchronize Translations	Synchronize fields for node-translated nodes	48
Node	Entity Translation	Translate fields; no translation set	51-54
Comment	Entity Translation	Translate fields; no translation set	56-57
User	Entity Translation	Translate fields; no translation set	58-59
Taxonomy	Entity Translation	Translate fields; no translation set	60
Taxonomy	Taxonomy Translation	Fixed option; assign language to vocabulary; terms are assigned the same language	77-78
Taxonomy	Taxonomy Translation	Localize option; localize terms; no translation set; term language is same as source language	78-79
Taxonomy	Taxonomy Translation	Translate option; translate terms; term translation set; assign language to term	79-80
Entity	Field Translation	Translate field settings (for example, help text)	80-81
Block	Block Languages	Assign language visibility to block	66
Block	Block Languages	Translate block title/body; no translation set	67-69
Menu	Menu Translation	Fixed Language option; assign language to menu; menu items are assigned same language	71
Menu	Menu Translation	Translate and Localize option; translate menu item; menu item translation set; assign language to menu item	72-73
Menu	Menu Translation	Translate and Localize option; localize menu item; no translation set; menu item language is same as source language	73

More multilingual modules

We've worked with many multilingual Drupal 7 modules, but certainly not all. Here are some additional modules that you might find useful. Not all modules tagged as "Multilingual" are included, so check out `drupal.org/project/modules` for more.

Interface

- **Administration Language**: `drupal.org/project/admin_language`
- **Consistent Language Interface**: `drupal.org/project/languageinterface`
- **Language Icons**: `drupal.org/project/languageicons`
- **Language Switcher**: `drupal.org/project/language_switcher`
- **Language Switcher Dropdown**: `drupal.org/project/lang_dropdown`
- **Views Language Switcher**: `drupal.org/project/views_lang_switch`

Content

- **GTranslate**: `drupal.org/project/gtranslate`
- **i18n_media**: `drupal.org/project/i18n_media`
- **Language Sections**: `drupal.org/project/language_sections`
- **Multi-Language Link and Redirect**: `drupal.org/project/multilink`
- **Translatable Regions**: `drupal.org/project/translatableregions`
- **TranslateThis Button**: `drupal.org/project/translate_this`
- **Translation Access**: `drupal.org/project/i18n_access`

Configuration

- **Apache Solr Multilingual**: `drupal.org/project/apachesolr_multilingual`
- **Context Locale Cookie**: `drupal.org/project/context_locale_cookie`
- **i18n Comments**: `drupal.org/project/i18n_comments`
- **IP to Locale**: `drupal.org/project/ip2locale`
- **Language Cookie**: `drupal.org/project/language_cookie`
- **Locale Cookie**: `drupal.org/project/locale_cookie`
- **Multilingual Forum**: `drupal.org/project/i18n`
- **Search API Entity Translation**: `drupal.org/project/search_api_et`

Admin tools

- **Language Assignment**: `drupal.org/project/languageassign`
- **Language Checker**: `drupal.org/project/langcheck`
- **Lingotek Collaborative Translation**: `drupal.org/project/lingotek`
- **Translation Management Tool**: `drupal.org/project/tmgmt`
- **Translation Overview**: `drupal.org/project/translation_overview`
- **Translation Table**: `drupal.org/project/translation_table`

Finding multilingual modules

How do you know if a module has multilingual support? This is not always obvious. If the module is tagged with the "Multilingual" category, then you can find it easily with the module search form at `drupal.org/project/modules`.

For other modules, first check out the module's project page and look for the right buzzwords such as **i18n**, **internationalization**, **multilingual**, **multilanguage**, **language**, **locale**, **localization**, and **translation**. If you still aren't sure, check the module's issue queue. There might be an issue for adding internationalization support. If there is one and it hasn't been fixed yet, you can click on the **FOLLOW** button on the top right of the page to keep track of the issue's progress. If progress has been made and there is a patch available, try out the patch and report your findings. That's what Drupal is all about!

Some modules don't need to do anything special to work on a multilingual website, so you can always just test the module to see if it works as expected. If it doesn't, then make sure to file an issue by following the issue report guidelines at `drupal.org/node/73179`.

Community resources

There are lots of great Drupal resources available. You can participate in the groups and forums, hop on IRC, read the documents and articles, and watch the videos!

Groups, forums, and IRC

- **Internationalization group**: `groups.drupal.org/i18n`
- **Translations group**: `groups.drupal.org/translations`
- **Translations forum**: `drupal.org/forum/30`
- **IRC channel**: `#drupal-i18n`

Documentation and guides

- **Multilingual Guide**: `drupal.org/documentation/multilingual`
- **HowTo: Basic Internationalization setup**: `drupal.org/node/1268692`
- **Translate Drupal to your language**: `drupal.org/contribute/translations`
- **Localization API**: `drupal.org/node/322729`
- **Module developer's guide (Multilingual support)**: `drupal.org/node/303984`
- **Internationalization module APIs**: `drupal.org/node/1114010`
- **Developer cheat sheet**: `hojtsy.hu/files/Drupal7TranslationCheatSheetv2.pdf`

Articles, videos, and more

- **Multilingual Drupal 7 articles**: `kristen.org/drupal7-i18n-articles`
- **Multilingual Drupal 7 videos/slides**: `kristen.org/drupal7-i18n-videos`
- **Multilingual Drupal 7 issues**: `kristen.org/drupal7-i18n-issues`
- **Multilingual Drupal 7 extra topics**: `kristen.org/drupal7-i18n-extra`

Getting involved

There are many ways to get involved with the Drupal community. Even if you are new, you can help others by answering questions in forums, groups, and IRC. If you are a designer or developer, write a cool theme or module and contribute it. If you know another language, translate text and submit it to `localize.drupal.org`.

Most communities have a local user group, so you can meet up with other Drupal users face-to-face. Then, of course, there are the fun DrupalCons and camps that happen regularly throughout the year. To learn more about getting involved, check out `drupal.org/getting-involved`.

What's up for Drupal 8?

The Drupal community is actively striving to improve Drupal each and every day. Many people have been hard at work on Drupal 8 since 2011. As mentioned previously, Gábor Hojtsy (`drupal.org/user/4166`) is heading up the Drupal 8 Multilingual Initiative (D8MI) with the number one goal to "make language support awesome in Drupal 8!"

If you review the D8MI plan and top priorities at `hojtsy.hu/d8mi`, you can see that there's plenty of work to do! You can help make Drupal 8 awesome. To get involved, check out the issue queue, hop on IRC for a meeting, or attend a code sprint.

Want more?

I tried to be thorough, but no doubt you'll have a question or topic that hasn't been covered in this book. No worries! Just send along your query to `kristen.org/contact`. I'll be regularly adding tips and tricks to my blog. For multilingual topics, you can find my relevant blog posts at `kristen.org/i18n`.

Index

D

E

F

G

taxonomy translation module 75, 110
Text field 53
t() function 12, 104
title module 109
Translate and Localize option 70
Translate Drupal to your language 114
Translate radio button 79
Translate tab 44, 47, 54, 68, 80
translation
  about 11
  automatic updates 27, 28
  contributing, to community 32, 33
  forum 113
  group 113
  interface 25-27
  interface translation, adding 29-32
  interface translation, fixing 29-32
  set 11
translation crowdsourcing 100
translation management
  and workflow 99
  content administration 99, 100
  custom workflow 101
translation management,
    contributed modules
  Lingotek Collaborative
      Translation module 100
  Translation Management Tool module 100
Translation Management Tool module 100
Translation mode section 71
Translation Redirect module 98
Transliteration module 94, 110

U

UI 11
und 11
URL alias field 93
URL method 22
use cases, example
  blog site 9
  company site 9
  demo site 10
  e-commerce site 9, 10
user interface. *See* UI
user method 22
users 58
Users may translate this field checkbox 58
users, non-node views 86, 87

V

variable translation module 108
view bulks operations 18
views
  about 18, 81
  language-specific views, creating 83
  multilingual views 81, 82
  nodes, using field translation 83, 84
  non-node views 84
  text 87
views slideshow 18

Thank you for buying
Drupal 7 Multilingual Sites

About Packt Publishing

Packt, pronounced 'packed', published its first book "*Mastering phpMyAdmin for Effective MySQL Management*" in April 2004 and subsequently continued to specialize in publishing highly focused books on specific technologies and solutions.

Our books and publications share the experiences of your fellow IT professionals in adapting and customizing today's systems, applications, and frameworks. Our solution based books give you the knowledge and power to customize the software and technologies you're using to get the job done. Packt books are more specific and less general than the IT books you have seen in the past. Our unique business model allows us to bring you more focused information, giving you more of what you need to know, and less of what you don't.

Packt is a modern, yet unique publishing company, which focuses on producing quality, cutting-edge books for communities of developers, administrators, and newbies alike. For more information, please visit our website: www.packtpub.com.

About Packt Open Source

In 2010, Packt launched two new brands, Packt Open Source and Packt Enterprise, in order to continue its focus on specialization. This book is part of the Packt Open Source brand, home to books published on software built around Open Source licences, and offering information to anybody from advanced developers to budding web designers. The Open Source brand also runs Packt's Open Source Royalty Scheme, by which Packt gives a royalty to each Open Source project about whose software a book is sold.

Writing for Packt

We welcome all inquiries from people who are interested in authoring. Book proposals should be sent to author@packtpub.com. If your book idea is still at an early stage and you would like to discuss it first before writing a formal book proposal, contact us; one of our commissioning editors will get in touch with you.

We're not just looking for published authors; if you have strong technical skills but no writing experience, our experienced editors can help you develop a writing career, or simply get some additional reward for your expertise.

Drupal 7 Multi Sites Configuration

ISBN: 978-1-84951-800-0   Paperback: 100 pages

Run multiple website from a single instance of Drupal 7

1. Prepare your server for hosting multiple sites

2. Configure and install several sites on one instance of Drupal

3. Manage and share themes and modules across the multi-site configuration

Drush User's Guide

ISBN: 978-1-84951-798-0   Paperback: 140 pages

A practical guide to Drush, Drupal's command line interface, helping you work with your Drupal sites more effectively

1. Stop clicking around administration pages and start issuing commands straight to your Drupal sites

2. Write your own commands, hook in to alter existing ones and extend the toolkit with a long list of contributed modules

3. A practical guide full of examples and step-by-step instructions to start using Drush right from Chapter 1

Please check **www.PacktPub.com** for information on our titles

Drupal 7

ISBN: 978-1-84951-286-2   Paperback: 416 pages

Create and operate any type of website quickly and efficiently

1. Set up, configure, and deploy a Drupal 7 website

2. Easily add exciting and powerful features

3. Design and implement your website's look and feel

4. Promote, manage, and maintain your live website

Drupal 7 Module Development

ISBN: 978-1-84951-116-2   Paperback: 420 pages

Create your own Drupal 7 modules from scratch

1. Specifically written for Drupal 7 development

2. Write your own Drupal modules, themes, and libraries

3. Discover the powerful new tools introduced in Drupal 7

4. Learn the programming secrets of six experienced Drupal developers

5. Get practical with this book's project-based format

Please check **www.PacktPub.com** for information on our titles

18180756R00074

Made in the USA
Lexington, KY
18 October 2012